"This beautifully written and moving memoir of a woman's search to find her authentic self, buried beneath decades of social conditioning and academic prejudice, will resonate with those who share her longing to recover her early reverence for the natural world and to direct their gifts and experience to serving it. In a culture immersed in the fascination with technology, we have forgotten our origins and our profound relationship with the planet. This book offers hope, inspiration and support to all those who, aware of disaster staring us in the face, are searching for courage and insight into how to respond. A timely and most valuable contribution to the greatest challenge of our times."

— Anne Baring, author of *The Dream of the Cosmos: a Quest for the Soul*

"Jennifer Browdy has chosen to write what she calls a 'purposeful memoir....' Her choice can inspire us all to see how our lives have been hijacked or distracted from what we most deeply desire, and how we can reclaim our lives for the sake of life on Earth."

— Joanna Macy, author of *Coming Back to Life* and *Active Hope: How to Face the Mess We're In Without Going Crazy*

"She documents the process of waking up to the world around us and she demonstrates how vibrant and rewarding an engaged life can be."

— Mary Pipher, author of *Reviving Ophelia* and *The Green Boat: Reviving Ourselves in Our Capsized Culture*

WHAT I
FORGOT

...AND WHY I REMEMBERED

A Journey to
Environmental Awareness and Activism
Through Purposeful Memoir

WHAT I
FORGOT

...AND WHY I REMEMBERED

A Journey to
Environmental Awareness and Activism
Through Purposeful Memoir

JENNIFER BROWDY

Green
Fire
Press

Housatonic
Massachusetts

Cover photo by Jennifer Browdy
Cover and page design by Anna Myers Sabatini

Library of Congress Control Number: 2016909000
ISBN: 978-0-9861980-4-5

Green Fire Press
PO Box 377 Housatonic MA 01236

Some of the names in this memoir have been
changed to protect the privacy of individuals.

Dedicated with love and gratitude to my parents,
Joe and Sue Browdy, companions of a lifetime,
who have taught me so much about love, generosity,
commitment and perseverance

CONTENTS

WHAT I FORGOT

FORGOT

...AND WHY I REMEMBERED

A Journey to
Environmental Awareness and Activism
Through Purposeful Memoir

EARTH/WATER/ FIRE/AIR

EMBARKING ON THE ELEMENTAL JOURNEY OF PURPOSEFUL MEMOIR

Back in the 1970s, when I was a kid, the feminist slogan "the personal is political" was a mantra for social revolution, but in my East Coast American circle few people I knew were especially revolutionary. Most of us just went with the flow of the dominant culture into which we were born—the one that promised success and good fortune to those who played by the rules and didn't rock any boats. Very few of us realized that the rules were being set by people who cared little for anything beyond their personal wealth, or that our own gilded and much-vaunted American lifestyles were to blame for a whole host of local and global social and environmental problems. In those days, the term "carbon footprint" hadn't yet been invented, and the environmental movement wore the face of a weeping Indian standing in road-side garbage. If we worried at all about how many miles our car could get out of a gallon of gas, the concern was based on our wallets, not on the impact of our collective greenhouse gases—another term that had yet to gain any traction.

Slowly, as we stepped into the new millennium, even my distracted, hyper-busy, self-centered generation began to realize that not only was the personal political, it was planetary too—and every choice we made mattered. The chemicals used in food production and industry poisoned us right along with our natural environment. Who couldn't name dozens of friends and relatives who were battling cancer, or had already succumbed? We all religiously got our mammograms and colonoscopies and started buying organic food, but we have been slow to realize that we cannot mend our own health unless we attend to the health of the planet as a whole. Reluctant to fully apprehend the planetary consequences of our personal and political choices, we have preferred not to see how the stepped-up pace of "natural disasters" in the first few years of the 21st century—the floods and the wildfires, the hurricanes and the tsunamis, the heat waves in summer and the frigid temperatures in winter—are a direct result of the ever-increasing impact of all of us humans on the planet, seven billion and counting, burning fossil fuels, clear-cutting forests, wiping out sea life and farming with life-destroying, soil-depleting chemicals. For a smart species, we can be pretty dense.

If we truly acknowledged our responsibility for the destabilization of our beautiful, battered planet, we would have to seriously contemplate change—a scary, dirty word for people like me, who have been enjoying a very comfortable ride here in the heart of the American empire.

Social revolutions are most often started by people who have nothing to lose. It's no wonder that those of us privileged folks who have been on the receiving end of the planet's bounty our whole lives would much rather just tune out. Even when we read the alarming reports about global warming, glacier melt, rising seas and acidified oceans, we are only half paying attention. The other part of our brain is engaged with the much more pleasurable activities of planning our next vacation or reshuffling the stocks in our portfolio.

I know this is true, because I lived the first 50 years of my life this way, treading the deeply rutted grooves of habit each day, following pathways laid down for me by earlier generations. No revolutionary, I just went with the flow of my culture, conforming to expectations, trying to live decently within the established boundaries. Like a small stream flowing into a mighty river, I allowed myself to be caught up in strong cultural currents that carried me along comfortably enough—though the price of the ride turned out to be the suppression of my own deepest knowledge and awareness.

A wise man named Socrates taught that we come into this world already knowing everything we need to know, but at birth we forget this prior knowledge and have to spend a great part of our lives trying to remember, or learning it anew. As a small child, what I knew was that I loved nothing more than to wander the woods and fields around my country home, communing with the trees and the flowers, the birds and the deer. Gradually, as I became an adolescent, I forgot how essential this close communion with the Earth was; I joined the stream of my tribe of affluent, cosmopolitan New Yorkers and was carried a long way before I finally picked up my head, spluttering, and realized that the dominant cultural tide was sweeping me, along with everyone else, into very dangerous waters indeed.

In writing this memoir I seek to discover how it was that I lost the instinctive reverence for the natural world that I had as a child; how I was socialized into playing the role of the cooperative, quiet woman in my time and place; and how I kept my head above water with the helping hands of stronger women, whose fierce words threw me lifelines that encouraged me to remember and honor what I knew as a child. I write first to acknowledge and then to question the way I trusted the seductive, destructive cultural frameworks that structured my life, including the basic institutions of education, career and marriage. I write to face the fact that I have lost a lot of time chasing success understood in conventional terms, which I now know will only be fool's gold if it is won at the expense of future generations. I write out of a deep and abiding hope that there is still time to embrace the personal, political and planetary transformations that are needed to see humanity through these perilous times into a brighter, more balanced future.

Each of us alive today is a spark of the *anima mundi*, the soul of our world, and she is calling on us now to step into our potential as the stewards of the planet. We cannot afford to wait for a charismatic leader; there will be no miracles. But there is an opportunity now, thanks to our amazing technological prowess as a species, for all of us to participate as never before in a global cultural shift that can catapult us into a new, more ecologically balanced relationship with our planet. It is possible that we will finally begin to realize, as Joanna Macy says so eloquently, that "the world is our body"; that when we damage and destroy the world, we are damaging and destroying ourselves and our collective future on the planet. It is still possible for us to change.

I offer my story in the hope that it will get you thinking about your own: about what you knew as a child; how your cultural socialization has shaped you; and how the challenges you may have faced as an adult helped you sharpen your understanding of your passions and carve out some new channels, independent of your upbringing. This is the elementary journey of purposeful memoir, looking back at where we've come from in order to understand where we are now and where we want to go, individually and collectively, on this beloved planet we call home.

I have used the four primary elements to structure my journey:

- Earth, the childhood ground of our being;

- Water, the cultural streams we enter as young adults;

- Fire, the passions we develop and also the crucible of life's challenges;

- and Air running through it all in the form of reflections and commentary from my current vantage point.

I think of purposeful memoir as a sort of purification ritual conducted through writing; a process of excavating and exorcising the past in order to bridge the way towards a transformative future. I write in the hope that galvanized by this process, we may go forward together with new strength and insight to become the agents of change the world surely needs now.

AIR

MEMORIES OF ABUNDANCE

One of my favorite stories in childhood was Leo Lionni's *Frederick*. It's a simple story about industrious little mice who work hard all summer to store away enough nuts and seeds for the winter. Nothing threatens them, and they are happy and contented in their work, making it into a kind of play. Frederick, however, is different. While his family gathers nuts and seeds, he just sits on a rock and communes quietly with nature. They give him dirty looks, thinking he is lazy, and accusing him of not working hard enough for the family. Frederick defends himself, saying that he is doing a different kind of work: gathering sunshine, colors and words for the long cold winter.

Late in the winter, the mouse family is faced with hunger as the last of their supplies are eaten up. It's then that Frederick comes into his own, sharing his own harvest of the images and sensations that he gleaned during the summer, conveying spiritual sustenance to his family to get them through the lean time of hardship.

Like Frederick, I was sometimes made to feel guilty as a child for sitting quietly out in the woods rather than pitching in to clean the house or rake the lawn. And like Frederick, I had an intuitive sense that the beauty of nature could sustain us just as much as her bounty, if only we took the time to drink deeply, with all our senses, from her well. Today the story of Frederick has even more resonance for me, as our planet teeters on the edge of violent social and environmental catastrophe. There may come a time, sooner than many of us care to imagine, when the nuts and seeds will start to run out, and we humans will be hungry. Like Frederick, what I have to offer are my words, as spiritual nourishment to strengthen our hearts and prepare us to face the lean seasons that may be coming.

EARTH

ON HOME GROUND

Earliest childhood: I am lying snuggled next to Mommy in her big bed, both of us cozy under the thick red quilt that glows in a pool of warm yellow lamplight. In rhythmic, musical tones, Mommy reads me the mesmerizing story Goodnight Moon. *As she reads and turns the pages slowly, I am drawn into each richly detailed illustration, and can feel myself settling down just like the bunny in the book, snug and warm, quietly drifting down into a safe, secure sleep. Goodnight house. Goodnight mouse. Goodnight stars. Goodnight air. Goodnight voices. Everywhere.*

My childhood was anchored by the ritual of the nightly bedtime story. One or the other of my parents read to me every evening and even as a very small child I had an extensive library of books: Dr. Seuss, P.D. Eastman, Maurice Sendak and many more. Besides *Goodnight Moon*, my other early favorite was Virginia Lee Burton's *The Little House*, which perfectly expressed the way I felt as a child who moved constantly between city and country. I could empathize with the deep unhappiness of the Little House when she was squeezed and oppressed by the dark, dirty, gray skyscrapers that grew up all around her; and when she moved back to the country, to a green, flower-strewn hillside surrounded by apple trees next to a shining blue brook, I could feel in my own heart the lightness of spirit and total peacefulness that overtook her as she relaxed in the clear air of the quiet, sun washed hill.

Unlike the Little House, who only had to move once, I spent my childhood shuttling constantly back and forth between the big city—where my father worked, my mother had her pottery studio and my brother and I went to school—and the country house in upstate New York where my family spent weekends and summers. Because I was never fully immersed in either of these spheres, I saw both through outsider's eyes, and was able to perceive the profound contrasts between the urban and rural environments.

I had a deep-seated, wordless aversion to living in the concrete canyons of Manhattan, where the sunlight could reach some streets only at high noon, and the only wild creatures around were grimy pigeons, sparrows and rats. I hated seeing the stunted, starved little trees that were planted in tiny, dirty squares left open in the concrete; they would struggle valiantly for a season or two and then give up, their skeletons standing propped in their iron cages until the next victims were stuck into the ground in their place. I hated crowds, and the feeling of vulnerability I always had as a small girl-child in Manhattan. Although my family lived very comfortably, to me living in Manhattan still felt like being trapped in a frightening concrete prison. Each week I waited impatiently for Friday night when we'd get in the car to go to the country, where the air was rich and cool, the trees tall and sheltering, and the whole landscape was buzzing with peaceful, benevolent life.

The property my grandparents had bought when I was born spanned 14 acres of open meadows and new-growth woods, studded with magnificent old sugar maples. The rocky land had been used as dairy cow pasture and was mostly thicket when my grandparents bought it in 1961, with just the back field, which we called the Lower Meadow, open and grassy from being mowed for hay every year. Set in a beautiful clearing in the center of five stately old maples was a small, three-season hunting cabin, which my grandparents renovated, bringing in electricity and plumbing, adding a bathroom, and putting in a refrigerator and a stove. There were two bedrooms; one for my grandparents, and one for me. My parents slept on the sofa bed on the sun porch with its big glass windows, which brought the woodland surroundings up close.

In the country, at least in terms of human society, I was in fact an outsider, a city person, an oft-resented "weekender." But I spent very little time in human society when I was in the country—that wasn't what I was there for. I always rose at first light on Saturday and Sunday, so that by dawn I could be dressed and outside, whatever the season or weather. I loved nothing more than to stand on the crest of the ridge looking east in the morning, to watch the sun's slow and steady appearance over the mountains, breathing deeply of the sweet air and listening to the bird songs welcoming the approach of day. I, who was so fearful walking the city streets, wandered through the woods by myself without any fear, following deer paths, streams and old stonewalls to secret glens high up on the mountains surrounding our house.

Walking through the woods, I entered a kind of waking dream-state. With my senses heightened and zinging with clarity of perception, I lost all track of time and felt at one with the pulsating life around me. I would often stay out from before dawn to late morning, when inevitably the distant honking of a car horn would startle me out of my reverie—it was my brother, sent to signal me, in those pre-cell-phone days, to return home for lunch.

My parents accepted my idiosyncrasies without question, allowing me the freedom to be myself in the country in a way that was impossible for me in the city. They took no heed when I stood for hours next to the bird feeder, until at last the little chickadees began to land on me freely, thinking me just another part of the inanimate landscape. They said nothing when I brought a chair outside on a day of heavy fog and sat on a hill to feel the cold, wet mist enveloping me, or when I spent hours sitting high up in my favorite maple tree, the one I named Cricket, stretching out my whole length along a limb to feel the swaying of the wind in the branches, becoming one with the branch and the tree.

I was a strange child. I knew it even then, because no one was like me, not even my best friend Allison. No one in my experience seemed to care as deeply as I did about the sweet, sharp creatures that shared our country home—the chickadees, the deer, the chipmunks, the owls and the bats. As a child, walking in the woods, I felt like I was always very close to being able to communicate with these creatures. I would stand stock-still upon encountering a deer in the forest, and slowly the deer would come towards me, step by cautious step, sniffing curiously to see what this strange still being might be, until finally, realizing I was a human, it would stamp and snort in warning and flee, white tail bobbing into the leafy green. At night when I heard an owl calling, I would go out and stand in the darkness, listening with all my senses, hoping that it might swoop close enough so that I could feel the wind rushing in its feathers.

In the summer, sitting by the pond, I would watch the fish swimming easily beneath the surface, and try to project myself inside one and imagine what it would be like to be fully immersed in that watery world. Or I would lie for hours in the tall grass in the spring under the blooming apple trees, entranced by the loud busy droning of the bees as they made their way from blossom to blossom, wondering what it would be like to be able to bury my whole head inside a fragrant bloom and come away dusty with golden pollen.

It is still dark. A four-year-old child, I hop out of bed and join Grandma Fannie in the kitchen of our little country cottage. She moves about quietly, boiling water to pour into two white china cups, into which she has spooned a little heap of the fragrant Postum she and I both love. We don't say much as we sip the hot drink and slip into our jackets just as the sun rises, Grandma slinging her binoculars around her neck as she follows me out the side door into the bright slanting sunshine of an early spring morning. The forest around our house is lit up with the neon green of new leaves and pulsing with a riot of musical birdcalls.

Grandma walks slowly and a little stiffly, pausing to bend over a wildflower or to peer up into the branches of a tree to locate the source of a persistent warble. Patiently, she teaches me to recognize and name all the birds we see on our "nature walks."

We pore over the bird books at home, and create long lists of all the birds we've sighted, neatly organized by date on big pieces of poster board. Swallows, gold and purple finches, phoebes, red-winged blackbirds, red-tailed hawks, juncos, chickadees, titmice, blue jays, cardinals, orioles, flickers, woodpeckers, kingfishers, mallard ducks, great blue herons, sparrows, starlings, cowbirds, grackles and crows...I know them all by sight and sound and can recite their names like poetry long before I learn to read.

Grandma also teaches me the colorful common names of the wildflowers that grow in profusion in the woods and fields around our house: jill-over-the-ground, jack-in-the-pulpit, goldenrod, star grass, St. John's wort, bladderwort, bloodroot and many more. She shows me how to pull off a single red and yellow petal from the wild columbines that cling tenaciously to the mossy rocks in the woods, and carefully suck at the tiny globe at the end of the petal to taste the sweet nectar collected inside. Later in the summer she'll show me the Monarch caterpillars feasting on the milkweed down by the pond, and we'll admire the honeybees as they make their way busily through the strongly scented mauve flowers of the wild bee balm. The names of all the wildflowers resound in my memory in Grandma's voice, along with the sound of her disapproving cluck when I hold up in my chubby hand a handful of purple violets and dandelions for her to admire. "Why must you always pick?" she asks irritably. And from that day on, at least when I'm with her, I never do.

Grandma Fannie, my father's mother, was a high school biology teacher by profession and a naturalist by vocation. I wish she had also known the medicinal uses of the wild plants she could identify, but she herself was new to the land she loved, her knowledge wide but shallow. She grew up on the Lower East Side of Manhattan at the turn of the 20th century, the daughter of Yiddish-speaking immigrants from the terror-stricken Russian-Polish Jewish *shtetls*. Grandma earned her B.A. and Master's in biology from Hunter College back in the 1930s, when it was still rare for women to go past high school, let alone major in the sciences. She and my Grandpa Phil were radicals in their youth: the children of immigrant garment workers, they were active in the New York workers' movement that gained momentum in the wake of the tragic Triangle Shirtwaist Factory fire of 1911. Grandpa went so far as to join the Communist Party, and together they went on a daring, romantic trip to Russia by ship in the 1920s, to check out the results of the Bolshevik Revolution for themselves. Scandalously, they were not yet married at the time.

By the time I knew her, there was little trace left of the idealistic, fiery young girl my grandmother once was. She and Grandpa had been caught up in the McCarthy witch hunts; he had been forced out of his job as a high school history teacher, and during the 1950s, when my father was a boy, they made several exploratory forays into

Mexico, where many blacklisted Americans were fleeing in those years. Fear of persecution, brought to a fever pitch by the execution of the Rosenbergs in 1953, formed the backdrop of my father's childhood, along with Grandma Fannie's persistent depression, for which she was hospitalized, medicated and given electroshock treatments. None of this was ever talked about when I was growing up; I didn't learn about this part of my family history until I was well into adulthood.

My father did talk about the happier aspects of his childhood: playing stickball in his Brooklyn neighborhood, following the Dodgers devotedly, and enjoying his status as the beloved only child in his family. He learned to play the guitar and sang Woody Guthrie and Pete Seeger union songs at the Jewish Federation camp where he and my mother met as teenagers; then he went to Oberlin and NYU Law and joined the postwar boom as an ambitious real estate lawyer at one of Manhattan's most illustrious firms. Grandpa Phil, meanwhile, finished off his working life as an analyst for a big investment firm. I remember him as being rather sad and reserved, smoking smelly cigars for a while, then a fragrant pipe, and then nervously keeping his mouth busy with butterscotch Lifesavers, which I loved to fish from his pockets. How they all felt about this family drift from youthful idealism to full immersion in the most high-powered capitalist city on Earth, I still don't know.

Once retired, Grandma liked to keep busy by attending cultural events in the city and gardens or big house museums in the country. She took me several times to the New York City Ballet at Lincoln Center, where I fell in love with the long-legged, elegantly twirling dancers in their brilliantly colored costumes, creating mesmerizing kaleidoscopic patterns that seemed to flow right out of the soaring melodies and rhythms of the orchestra. In her old age, after Grandpa Phil passed away, Grandma moved from the big, gloomy apartment on Ocean Parkway, where my father had been raised, to a bright one-bedroom apartment in the Educational Alliance building on Henry Street on the Lower East Side, where nearly a century earlier her parents had settled after passing through Ellis Island. Grandma gave classes to other Alliance residents in Yiddish literature and poetry writing, and was constantly reading and writing. When we came to visit her on Sundays, taking her out for brunch at Coney Island or Ratner's, she would regale us with recitations of the humorous rhymes and short stories that she wrote out by hand, in pencil, in her lined notebook. My mother and father would nod politely, clearly not that interested in what she had to share. For my brother and me her topics often seemed foreign and hard to understand, but I loved to see how animated she became as she pulled out her notebook and began to read, and the way her bright blue eyes would crinkle with pleasure at the humorous dialogues of her characters.

While our new country house is being built, just down the hill from Grandma and Grandpa's cottage, we are staying for a few days at Christmastime with my parents' friends Aaron and Amelia Mitrani, in their old farmhouse in Ancram, New York. I am five years old and so excited when I wake up on Christmas morning to feel the solid, bulging weight of my stocking at the end of my bed. I empty it out gleefully, opening up the little presents and sorting the candies and chocolates into shiny heaps, to be savored later. Mommy is awake too, even though it's still pitch dark; together we go down the chilly stairway into the kitchen, where Amelia has lit a fire in the old cast-iron cook stove. The stove radiates a cozy band of heat, and I sit happily at the table beside it, listening to the quiet murmur of Mommy and Amelia talking. I sip my hot milk and hum a bar of "O Come All Ye Faithful," one of the many exultant Christmas carols we've been singing all week.

My breath catches as I look up and see a huge, glittering star shining brightly in the black sky, framed by the picture window. It's Venus, the Morning Star, Amelia tells me when I point it out excitedly. A perfect crescent moon hangs next to it in the velvety darkness, casting cold shadows on the snowy landscape just barely visible below. I'm fascinated by the way the star and the moon hang together so low and bright, almost touching, and feel a strange magnetic pull emanating from them, penetrating into my core. The contrast between the close warmth of the kitchen and the cold *immensity of the starlit world beyond the window hits me with all the force of trumpeting angels.*

Aaron Mitrani was the director of the Jewish Federation summer camp for kids and seniors where my parents met as teenagers in the 1950s. My father was the music counselor, my mother the art counselor. The camp was built around a deep, cold lake, home to huge old snapping turtles and ancient bass and carp; in the early days of their romance, my parents were housed on opposite sides of the lake, and my mother would swim across at dusk to visit my dad, her strong, clean crawl making quick work of the crossing.

My parents broke up briefly while my dad was away at Oberlin and my mom was having fun as a bohemian student at Manhattan's lively High School of Music and Art. But in the end they came back together and were married in 1958, just a few days after my mom's 18th birthday; my dad was 21. While he was in law school at New York University, they lived in a special dorm for married graduate students on Washington Square West, my mom cooking on a hot plate and going down to swim in the ice-cold natural pool in the basement of the building, all that was left of Minetta Brook, which had once flowed peacefully across lower Manhattan to the river. My dad worked hard at his classes, joining the Law Review staff and receiving accolades from his teachers and peers, while my mom found her way to Greenwich House Pottery in the West Village and began the immersion in clay that would become one of her most deeply held passions.

Things got bumpy in 1961, when my dad was called up for military service amid the Cold War sabre-rattling between the USSR and the U.S., which was much more dangerous and frightening in a postwar landscape bristling with nuclear missiles. He went through basic training at Fort Dix, and then was sent down to a base in Georgia. I was conceived out of this *sturm und drang*, the baby whose presence would, hopefully, keep my father from being shipped out to war. Pregnant with me, my mom went down to Georgia, where, between the Southern military base wives, the overt racism and the giant cockroaches, she got a big dose of culture shock along with her constant morning sickness. She flew back to New York in a blizzard; her plane was diverted to Philadelphia, and she waited in the airport with her big belly and her newly acquired Dachshund, Inchy, until her frantic parents could arrange to pick her up and bring her back to Brooklyn.

I was born in Brooklyn Hospital just after the intense month-long standoff of the Cuban missile crisis, and just as Rachel Carson published *Silent Spring*. In keeping with the medical protocols of the time, my mom was anesthetized and unconscious for my birth, and she was given pills to dry up her milk; I was bottle-fed from birth. That year

My mom and me at the East River esplanade;
photo taken by my dad.

my dad started working at the big, glamorous law firm where he was to stay his entire career, and we moved to the Upper East Side, where my parents would live, in a series of apartments, for the next forty years. My mom continued to work in clay at the 92nd Street Y, and was fortunate to find a loving teenage babysitter in our next-door neighbor, Liza, with whom I quickly bonded.

What I don't remember from my first year of life

April 16, 1963: Martin Luther King Jr. is imprisoned during anti-segregation protests in Birmingham, Alabama and writes his seminal "Letter from Birmingham Jail," arguing that individuals have the moral duty to disobey unjust laws.

June 12, 1963: Mississippi's NAACP field secretary, 37-year-old Medgar Evers, is murdered outside his home.

August 28, 1963: About 200,000 people join the March on Washington, where Martin Luther King delivers his indelible "I Have a Dream" speech at the Lincoln Memorial.

September 15, 1963: Riots erupt in Birmingham following the deaths of four young African American girls attending Sunday school, killed when a bomb explodes at the Sixteenth Street Baptist Church.

November 22, 1963: President John F. Kennedy Jr. is assassinated.

The beat of violence, terror and inflamed emotions continued throughout my early childhood. I was sheltered from all of it, and yet, as a sensitive child who was very, very slow to separate from my mother, I felt her tension and fear as we walked the streets of Manhattan, and how all of it went away when we headed for the country on weekends. In the early years, before I started school, my mom and I used to go out in the morning twice a week and sit in our car, a little red Renault Dauphin, for two hours, during the alternate side of the street parking period. We just sat there and she read to me, or we talked. But one day as we were heading back home for lunch, my mom suddenly grabbed my hand and hurried me along towards the doorway of our apartment building, 181 E. 93rd Street. A raucous, rowdy group of Black boys was coming down the street, breaking the antennas off all the parked cars. As my mother hustled me inside I wondered what they would do with the fistfuls of metal antennas they were collecting, but I didn't ask. My mom was obviously upset, angry and fearful.

Mommy and I are living for the summer in a tent at camp, up on the hill above the lake, and Liza is

living with us too, taking care of me while Mommy
works as an art counselor. Daddy is working in the
city during the weeks, but he joins us on weekends.
On Saturday nights a big bonfire is lit in the clearing
in the center of the fragrant pinewoods, and we file
along the soft, needle-laden path to take our places
by the fire. Daddy is there with his guitar, and it's
his strong, passionate voice that leads the whole
group in song for the next few hours, as the darkness
deepens around the edges of the clearing, and stars
begin to glow overhead.

Which side are you on, boys, which side are you on?
My daddy was a miner, and I'm a miner's son.
And I'll stick with the union, 'til every battle's won.
Which side are you on, boys, which side on you on?

But when the magical musical interlude is over and
we make our way back to our tent by flashlight, I
must face the inevitable: the outhouse, in the dark.
I'm sure spiders or something worse will crawl up
out of the stinking hole and grab me as I sit on the
bench, pulling me downward. I whimper and cry and
get half-hysterical as Mommy stands in the doorway
holding my hand...and then it's over and I can crawl
into my sleeping bag and go back into the dream of
fire-lit clearings and voices singing their hearts out to
the stars.

    After a few weeks, Mommy starts taking me to
a friend's house to use the bathroom, because I'm so

entirely constipated. I don't like it there either—once there was a snake coiled around the water pipe, and there are spiders in the corners. But at least there is a real white porcelain toilet, and it doesn't smell. I hurry and try to do my business so that I can rejoin Mommy and Uncle Larry, who are laughing and talking out on the porch. I don't like feeling stuck.

My parents' good friend Larry was my first crush. I loved him wholeheartedly because of the loving attention he showered on me when we were together. Like Liza, he enjoyed talking with children, and made me feel like I was smart and interesting— like there was no one else in the room he'd rather be hanging out with. As the first child among my parents' friends, I got a lot of attention in those early years and I ate it up. When I went to nursery school at the United Nations School, I had little use for my peers; I was shy and reserved, keeping my own counsel and playing my own games.

When I was five, my brother was born. I remember lying on the bed with my mom in the last few weeks of her pregnancy; she would perch her ashtray on her big belly and it would shake with his kicks. She and my dad smoked cigarettes all through my childhood. I went through terrible agonies on the weekly car rides upstate, as they passed the lit cigarette back and forth between them in the front seat. Even on the coldest nights, I would crack the window and keep my nose to it like a dog. My hatred of cigarette smoke was another one of my idiosyncrasies, which my parents politely but firmly ignored.

It is the first day of kindergarten, my first day at a new school, P.S. 198 on 96th Street, a few blocks from home. I am filled with a sense of dread as Mommy walks me into the classroom, and begin crying miserably as she detaches herself from my clutching hands and walks firmly out of the room. I am left alone in a corner, tears streaming down my clenched, puckered face. All of a sudden a sweet-faced, golden-haired girl appears, a kindergartener like myself, but as relaxed and self-confident as I am shy and nervous. "Don't cry!" she says—"come, let's play!" Grabbing my hand, she pulls me over to the corner where the blocks are stored, and coaxes me into setting some up with her. Her enthusiasm is infectious, and soon I have forgotten my tears in the earnestness of our play. I have made my first real friend.

Imogen, or Imin as I called her, was my best friend in those crucial years of early childhood. Although I'd been to nursery school, I did not make any close friends there. I was much more interested in interacting with the adults I knew—my babysitter Liza, my doting Uncle Larry, and always, my mother—the one person I could not do without. Imin brought out something different in me, a new camaraderie that could only arise between peers.

She was fearless in the social situations that frightened me—basically, anything involving leaving my mother's side—and she had a light-hearted spirit that was always searching for the next good time, a welcome contrast to my seriousness. We were inseparable in kindergarten, first and second grade, and used to talk on the phone after school, playing memory games or talking "gibberish" together, our attempt at imitating the rapid-fire Puerto Rican Spanish that was ubiquitous in our schoolyard, since P.S. 198 drew a lot of its population from nearby Spanish Harlem.

After second grade, my parents moved down to 87th Street, into the P.S. 6 school district, and I lost regular contact with Imin, whose parents—British and Swedish—sent her to boarding school in England at age 10. I made new school friends, and in the country there was my friend Allison, who was my age and so similar to me in temperament and interests that I thought of her as a sister. But there were many times when I missed the confidence and light-heartedness of Imin, spinning gleefully in her own laughing orbit.

Dream Memory: 5 years old

I am standing in the hallway, peering into the dark living room of the apartment we lived in for my first six years. There is a strange gathering there, around a round table set up in the middle of the room: a group of men and women, none of them familiar to me, except for Mommy who is there too. They are all looking avidly at the object in the center of the table, and my gaze is drawn there too: it is a huge, glowing red ruby, the size of a basketball, multifaceted and glittering with a kind of internal light. Somehow I know that these are robbers, and they have stolen this ruby. I shrink back, not wanting them to see me. I don't understand what Mommy is doing there. Is she there under compulsion? Or is she part of the gang?

This is the only dream I have carried with me from my early childhood, intact with the shiver of fear it aroused in me, and the questions I still cannot answer. There was a sense of salivating over that ruby, the avidness of ownership, but also the sense that the ruby had its own kind of intelligence and purpose that could not be mastered by the humans gathered around it. This memory goes together with another from the same time and place, this one not a dream:

I am standing behind the dusty, dingy drapes in the living room with Imin, looking out the window at the quiet alley between our apartment building and the next one down the block. We never go into that alley, but it has some spindly trees that manage to grow there despite the lack of sunlight, and I am always attracted to the leafy branches and the sparrows whose cheerful warbling echoes between the brick buildings.

Suddenly our attention fixes on a man who is climbing up the ladders of the metal fire escapes of the building across the way. We've never seen anyone climb those fire escapes before, and watch, curious. He goes in through an open window, and comes out a few minutes later, carrying a shopping bag that looks heavy. Weighed down by the shopping bag, he starts to make his way more slowly down the fire escape. I run to tell Mommy. "A man is on the fire escape across the alley! He's stealing!" She is busy talking with Imin's mother and looks at me blankly, not understanding what I'm saying. By the time I get her to come look out the window, the man has disappeared and I am disappointed that she doesn't seem to believe me.

But later that week I am vindicated, as word goes around the apartment building that there has been a rash of thefts; tenants are advised to keep the windows adjoining the fire escapes locked. The fire escape in our apartment is outside my bedroom window, right next to my bed. I am glad that the window is barred with locked metal gates, but I still feel a little uneasy, and keep my curtains closed.

One morning around this time, I actually accomplish something I had wanted to do for a long time: I manage not to move when I wake up, so I can "see" how I look when I'm asleep. While I'm lying very still, thinking about being asleep, a ray of sunshine comes *in through the grimy glass, the locked gate and the drawn curtains of the window by my bed. As I watch, fascinated, the air in the ray of sun comes alive with small twirling motes of dust that are entirely invisible in the rest of the room. I feel like I am being drawn into the glowing ray of sunshine...I become one of those lazily twirling motes, rising up into the air above my small, still body, lying just as it did while I was asleep under the bedspread with the blue and white heart pattern that Mommy made for me. I am safe.*

The summer my brother turned one and I was five and a half, we moved into our new little country house, an 800-square-foot octagonal house built for my parents a short way down the hill from my

grandparents' cottage. It was designed by an enterprising young architect, Ed Loedy, who had just graduated from architecture school and was eager to try out his innovative ideas. When he couldn't find a builder to take on his odd-shaped, labor-intensive design, he spent a year building the house himself. It had a peaked roof lined with red cedar on the inside, a cool slate floor, and windows all around, protected from the sun by deep cedar overhangs. There were two small bedrooms, a kitchen, a bathroom and a living room, all oddly shaped because of the octagonal walls; there was no basement or attic, but there were plenty of closets and shelves for storage. Because of the high central roof and all the windows, the house felt bigger than it was—your gaze was always being pulled outwards through the windows into the woods and fields. Towards the south, through the wall of sliding glass doors in the living room, there was a long rolling valley vista that met the distant line of the mountains and the sky.

That first summer, my mother began tending and shaping the land around the house, following her own instincts of landscaping and working almost entirely with hand tools. In front of the house, she raked out a big pile of topsoil and planted a small lawn. Beyond the lawn was an expansive swamp dogwood thicket, laced with black raspberries and bordered by a young maple forest on one side, and a few barely visible pine trees on the other, which my grandfather had planted as fingerlings when he first bought the land. Armed only with loppers, my mom began cutting down the thicket, a project that my brother and I joined in on when we were old enough to handle our own tools.

Once the thicket was gone, and grass had been seeded in its place, it became apparent that the house had been sited next to a huge limestone ledge, part of which was visible as outcroppings. My mother set to work with her shovel, hand rake and trowel, determined to create a rock garden out of that long, sloping rock ledge. That project provided a focus for many long summers to come, summers which she spent with me and my brother in the country while my father went back to the city to work during the weeks. I can see her standing, sweaty and red-faced at the end of a hot morning's work, with a fine layer of black earth coating her bare shoulders, drinking iced tea out of a tall green glass and surveying the ledge with a squinted sculptor's eye. She would be quietly exultant as her shovel and trowel gradually revealed new curves or deep, smooth walls of rock, a small, determined woman with a strong back and great patience, tracing out the rock with hand tools and as much love as if she were carving out the sweet, benevolent face and voluptuous body of the Earth Mother herself.

With the help of her parents, my Grandma Mildred and Grandpa Vic, Mommy also dug out a vegetable garden, in which she planted her morning coffee grounds and eggshells. The garden yielded crunchy sugar snap peas, big shiny zucchinis, and a tangle of tomato plants loaded down with plum, cherry and huge oxheart tomatoes. She also helped me create my own garden, a shady woodland garden under my climbing tree, Cricket, which I planted with columbine, ferns, may-apple and wild geranium, all carefully transplanted from the dappled woods around our property.

In time, every contour of the ten acres or so around the houses had felt the gentle touch of my mother's hands and yielded to the influence of her spades and trowels. Every young maple or oak grew there because she had judiciously allowed it to advance past sapling-hood. What had once been a rocky, harum-scarum cow pasture became, over the course of many years, an orderly oasis of verdant green lawns, perennial flower beds and raised vegetable gardens, with the long ridge of the rock garden sloping down through the middle of it all to the elegantly landscaped pool. This transformation formed one of the most intimate and persistent narratives of my childhood.

It's the long, slow twilit end of a long, slow, perfect summer day. As the sun goes down behind the mountain to the west of our little house, the pulsing chorus of crickets swells to a hypnotic pitch, and bats fly in swift circles around the peaked roof of the house, dipping and twirling like the aerial acrobats they are, intent on catching their dinner. I sit on the hillside above the rock garden, watching for the first fireflies in the meadow grass, blinking earthbound echoes of the stars coming out in the hazy summer sky overhead. In the deepening dusk, the lamps in the house glow with a warm golden light; I'm waiting until Mommy finishes putting my brother to sleep, so she can read me my bedtime story. Although I can read myself now, I still love Mommy to read to me, and we are in the middle of one of the most entrancing books I've ever encountered: The Voyage of the Dawn Treader, which we borrowed from the library. The idea of being pulled through a painting into another world delights me and tickles my imagination. But the truth is there is nowhere I would rather be than right here, on this peaceful darkening hillside, waiting for Mommy to call me in for bedtime.

In my childhood memories, the gentle, undulating peacefulness of the country contrasts sharply, over and over, with the angularity and discomfort of the city.

I'm in second grade and for some reason all of us kids are sitting on the floor in the gymnasium, waiting. I notice a ripple going down the line of kids towards me, and suddenly my neighbor has cupped her hands over my ear, leaning over to whisper urgently, "FUCK! Pass it on!" I look at her uncomprehendingly and she repeats it impatiently, gesturing at the next person in line and telling me again to "pass it on!" So I do, although I have no idea what I am saying. Later, at home, I ask my mother what FUCK means, and gather from her explanation that it is not a nice word—not a word I should say out loud.

Not long afterward, I am in the bathroom stall at school, and among lots of graffiti hearts with initials etched inside them, I read a large, angry proclamation: FUCK THE JEWS! My heart starts beating hard, and I can't stop staring at this. Why would someone hate the Jews enough to write this in public? Do they hate—me?

At some point during my childhood, I learned that because of my blonde hair and blue eyes, I could pass for something else besides Jewish. Since I wasn't automatically assumed to be Jewish on the basis of my looks, I often let the ambiguity ride unless directly asked for an explanation of my heritage. I wasn't embarrassed or ashamed to be Jewish, but I was instinctively afraid of being singled out, fearful that incomprehensible hatred would be thrown my way. When I could keep my ethnic heritage under the radar, I played it safe.

I felt somewhat justified in shrugging off my Jewishness because I did not grow up practicing the religion. My parents and grandparents celebrated Christmas as a secular American holiday focused on eating and gift-giving. Neither my father nor my grandfathers were bar mitzvahed; no one in my immediate family went to temple or practiced Judaism in any way. And yet Grandma Fannie's first language was Yiddish, and she often drew on Yiddish words to give emphasis to her English. My parents met at a Jewish Federation camp, and my father eventually served on the Board of that camp. He became a partner in a big Jewish-led law firm. We were and were not Jewish, in equal measure.

Not until much later did I realize that the camouflage afforded me by my fair features was a shield that was also, paradoxically, a mark of hatred embedded in my very genes. My blonde hair and blue eyes had to be the visible trace of grunted, wordless assaults on the terrified young bodies of my 19th century great-great-great grandmas, attacked and raped in their small Russian village, giving birth to children who bore the broad, soft features of the blond Russian and Polish overlords in the region, rather than the sharper, darker features of my Jewish forebears.

The science of epigenetics is just now beginning to explain empirically what I knew intuitively as a child: that we carry the memories of past traumas inscribed in us both psychologically and on a cellular level. This is the only way I can explain the fear that dogged my childhood, despite my parents' efforts—almost entirely successful—to shelter and cocoon me from any violence or danger.

Memories of awakening to gender as a girl-child

I am lying in the dark in my bed in the big bedroom at 1060 Park Avenue that I share with my brother. He is already asleep. It starts: the weird recurrent vision that I speak of to no one, of being tortured in a bed by evil men who bend over me malevolently. I seem to be hovering above my body, looking down on what is happening to the terrified young girl strapped to the bed. I don't feel pain, but I feel terror, absolute panic and gut-twisting fear, from which there is no escape. When I think about this scenario during the sunlit daytime hours, I am puzzled and a little ashamed. I tell no one about it, not even Mommy. There is nothing in my waking experience to explain or justify this nightmare. Where does it come from?

I'm standing with Mommy on the checkout line at the A&P on Lexington Avenue when an older woman comes up to us and says to Mommy, while patting me on the head, "What an adorable little boy! How old is he?"

I am completely taken aback. I am a girl! I want to shout at her. Mommy makes the correction, and the old lady moves on. But I remain in shock. I know the mistake was made because of the short haircut I've been getting, and from that moment, I vow I will never cut my hair again. I will let it grow and grow, just like a princess, so no one will ever mistake me for a boy again.

I am lucky that Liza's mother supplies me with beautiful flouncy dresses—the kind Mommy would never buy me. I love to try them on in front of the mirror: the black and white party dress with a polka-dot bodice and a silk sash; the plaid dress with a white lacy collar; the blue and white sailor dress with a red anchor embroidered on the side; and best of all my pink sequined gauzy tutu, which I love to wriggle into and dance.

What I really want is a pair of black patent leather Mary Janes and white tights to go with my outfits, like my friend Janine wears to school. But time after time Mommy and I come back from the StrideRite shoe store on Lexington Avenue with yet another pair of clunking black and white saddle shoes and boring blue Converse sneakers. Mommy tells me I have wide feet and Mary Janes don't come in wide sizes. I sulk and pout to no avail. There are no Mary Janes for me.

I am in 5th grade, walking alone on Park Avenue towards the 81st Street entrance to P.S. 6, minding my own business, not thinking about anything much. An older boy, maybe a sixth grader, is coming towards me on the street. As a well-trained New Yorker, I don't make eye contact with him, staring past him as I approach. But just as he comes abreast of me, he hisses in a harsh, abrasive tone, unmistakably aimed at me: "Fatso!"

Then he's past me, and I'm past him, and I don't turn around to hurl a corresponding insult at him; no, I feel his little poisoned arrow sinking deeply into me, bearing with it seeds of insecurity and self-consciousness that will take root and grow into a tangled, matted, wordless mass in my soul. I, who had never thought of myself as fat before, will bow my head before that savage indictment.

In the country, out in the woods, I could just be myself—not a girl, not a boy, not fat or thin, not pretty or ugly—just a pure, open-hearted channel through which the beauty of the natural world could flow. When I was very little I found my "spot" on the rock ledge just out of sight of the cottage, with tumbled glacial rocks ringing a small circular glade filled with long, silky wood grass studded with wild star flowers, violets and columbines in the spring. I'd go there to sit quietly and commune with the waving tree branches above me, or watch the ants moving busily along their paths among the stones. With each passing year, I expanded my self-imposed boundaries, first exploring every inch of our 14 acres, and then venturing further up the dirt road to the neighboring property, where a cold stream rushed along the foot of a mountainside girdled by old stone walls that led me up towards the ridge. In the late winter, when the trees were still bare, I'd be dazzled by the sight and sound of a red cardinal sitting on the highest branch of a silver-barked maple, silhouetted against an electric blue sky, singing his love songs at full volume, with all his heart. On rainy April mornings I'd delight to see the big noisy flocks of redwing blackbirds gathering in the trees around the stream and the pond, their trilling cries announcing the onset of spring. In full summer I'd sit dreamily on the rocks, sticking my bare feet in the stream and watching darting blue dragonflies. And in the fall I roamed the golden, red and orange hillside with special delight, loving the crisp fall air, the twirling colored leaves coming down and the crunch of the dried brown ones underfoot.

One fall, I was walking along as usual in the woods and all of a sudden was startled by the loud report of a gunshot, right near me. I ran to the streambed and crouched against the bank, hiding while several more shots whizzed by. I was both furious and frightened, imagining the bullets finding their target in the soft brown hide of one of my deer friends, and fearful that some uncouth hunter might step out of the woods and threaten me, too. Fuming and anxious, I waited a long time after the last gunshot sounded before making my way hurriedly home. The woods would be off limits to me now until after the end of the hunting season in December.

On the Friday before Christmas, Daddy leads us in singing all of our favorite folk songs as we wend our familiar way up the long dark highway. Our blue Buick LeSabre is packed to capacity with shopping bags of presents and food, and bulging suitcases full of wool sweaters and snow pants. I hang on the back of the front seat, singing lustily in Daddy's ear, showing off how I know all the words, sometimes even better than he does!

Finally we swing on to our road; it's a dark, cold night, with cascades of glittering stars overhead, and a deep blanket of snow carpeting the ghostly fields and woods. At the bottom of our driveway, Daddy slows to a stop and gives a little exclamation of annoyance. The snow lies thick and untouched over the steep driveway. Our neighbor Jack must have forgotten to plow us out. Daddy backs up to get a running start and barrels into the driveway, hoping to at least get the car far enough into the drifts to be off the road. After a few tries he succeeds, and I spring out of the car, pulling on my winter coat and stuffing my pants into the tops of my snow boots. There had been no snow at all in the city, so these deep drifts are a surprise. I bask in the quiet, serene night-time scene as my parents begin unloading the numerous bags and parcels from the car and schlepping them up the driveway to the house, pushing through the thigh-high snow. They have to carry my little brother to the house, too—the drifts are too deep for him to walk through.

While Mommy fumbles with the door key in the darkness, I gaze up at the stars winking through the bare tree limbs, knowing that in a moment she'll be inside, flicking on the electric lights that will drown out the stars. Soon the bags are piled in the living room, the electric heaters are pinging cheerily, and my parents take their bottle of Aquavit out of the freezer and pour themselves each a companionable shot. Wanting to block out the kitchen light, I close the door of the bedroom I share with my brother, climb into my bunk bed and fall asleep with one eye half-open, trying to watch the slow progress of Orion as it wheels over the big maple tree outside my window. I can never seem to stay awake long enough to see the movement of the constellations. Before I know it, I'm asleep.

Those early Christmases always unfolded in the same way. We would arrive in the country late on a Friday night, often having stopped along the way to pick up a Christmas tree that my parents strapped tightly to the car roof. The next day, we'd bring in the tree, set it up in its stand, and together wind on the lights and hang the decorations. The little house would fill with the fragrant scent of pine needles, along with the delicious smells of my mother's holiday cooking: savory Janssen's Temptation potatoes in cream sauce with anchovies, Christmas ham roasted in mustard sauce, and endless gingerbread cookies—all recipes she learned from Imin's Swedish mom, Kirsten. My brother and I would hang our handmade stockings on the door handles and wait impatiently for Christmas Eve, spending our time outside sledding down the driveway, or building snowmen on the front lawn who peered into the house with their black pebble eyes, their long carrot noses rakishly askew.

Somehow my mom would find a way to hide all the voluminous shopping bags of gaily wrapped presents, leaving the decorated tree bare underneath until the crowning glory of the holiday: the moment early on Christmas morning when I would wake up before anyone else and creep into the living room in my bare feet, to see, like a shining mirage of treasure, the tree heaped about with packages and parcels of every size and shape, glittering with shiny wrapping paper and big frilly bows. Much as I burned with curiosity to know what was inside the packages, I also wanted to savor the anticipation; I contented myself with opening up the small, funny presents in the bulging stocking at the foot of my bed while I waited for my mom to wake up and start making the coffee. Not until we were all four assembled could the great unwrapping ceremony joyfully begin.

It was the winter of my eighth year when that sense of limitless abundance hit a sudden roadblock.

It is a Sunday afternoon in late January, and a dark gray storm cloud has settled down on the snowy mountains. There is tension in the air as my parents work methodically to pack up the car and close down our little country house, loading in the suitcases, shopping bags of food, armloads of winter coats, Inchy the dachshund, my two-year-old brother, and me. Mommy had been arguing to stay put until morning, but Daddy is determined to get back to the city, so he won't be late for work the next day. We head towards the highway, and before we've even gotten out of town we hit an icy patch and our Buick LeSabre does a complete 360. My father struggles to get us pointed back in the right direction. My mother grips his arm, white-knuckled, and asks him again to turn back, but he is sure the highway will be better, and we continue on in silence.

My brother and I have both fallen asleep in the gloom of the late afternoon only to be awakened by a sudden change in the smooth rhythm of our forward motion. Before I know what is happening, there is a big jolt, and I've landed on the floor of the back-seat. My brother, too, is tumbled down onto the floor, landing on top of Inchy, who yelps and struggles to get out of the way. Mommy turns around in her seat, reaching for us and shouting "My babies!" and there is a heartbeat of silence before we hear an engine roar next to us and feel another big jolt as the car behind us slides headlong into my mother's door. As my brother wakes up and begins to cry, I say mechanically, "Yes, I'm all right, Mommy," and gaze in horror at the blood dripping from my father's chin, where he banged it into the steering wheel when we crashed into the car ahead of us. We sit frozen in an instant that has all the qualities of a nightmare, until the flashing *red police lights show up behind us and it's time to get out of the car.*

It was a seven-car pile-up on an icy stretch of highway near Westchester. The Buick was totaled, but we all seemed to be OK, except that my mother was unable to lift her foot into the back of the state police car when the trooper gave us a ride over to the hospital. In the emergency room, my father got some stitches in his chin and leg; my brother and I were fine. But my mom was not fine. The doctors pulled a curtain around her gurney and we were not even able to say goodbye as they wheeled her off in a hurry for an x-ray. My brother and I followed Dad out into the hospital lobby, where Inchy was waiting along with all our bags and suitcases. The trooper was going to give us a ride to a nearby motel for the night. As my father grabbed one of the shopping bags of food, the handles broke, the bag fell, and a half-gallon of milk opened up and spilled all over the shiny hospital linoleum. We left the mess behind for someone else to clean up.

Because she had twisted around in her seat to check on us, exposing her back, my mother's lower vertebrae had been crushed by the car that crashed into her door. While she stayed at the hospital for two weeks, my brother and I were cared for by Mildred, the housekeeper of my babysitter Liza's family, along with other friends and relatives. My dad went to work as usual, and came home for dinner as usual, and did not say much to us about this dreadful turn of events. I was in shock—such a deep sense of shock that I don't even remember crying. It was as if all my tears and fears were suspended in some kind of emotional deep-freeze, waiting for what would happen next.

Finally, my mom came home, but she was confined to her bed, trussed in a steel-rimmed corset. The doctors told her she might not walk again, a prospect she firmly refused to acknowledge. Slowly she healed, and she walked, and she went back to the normal routines of her life, including gardening and potting and toting heavy bags down to the car and up to the country again, on a highway freed from the clutches of winter. One more memory from that time haunts me: *I come in from school to find Mommy, as usual, lying in bed propped up on her pillows. She has her reading glasses on, and she is working on a piece of brown felt, embroidering it freestyle with golden trees, orange leaves and red mushrooms—a forest scene. I watch, fascinated, as her tiny stitches and knots gradually take form. I wish I could go away with my mother into that magical forest and never come back.*

After the accident, I became an even more fearful, worried sort of child, neurotically attached to my mother. I had always been reluctant to be separated from her, but as the years went by, the fear of losing her intensified and became paralyzing. I did not have the same fears about my father; I could watch him go off to work each morning dispassionately, and wait calmly for him to return home for dinner. It was my mother on whom my fears fixated obsessively. I used to interview her each morning before I left for school, wanting to know what her routine would be during the day so that in case she turned up missing, I would have some information to report to the police. I insisted that she take some "mugging money" with her when she walked over to the 92nd Street Y for her Tuesday night pottery class—a $20 bill tucked into her jeans pocket, "just in case." I would watch her from the window as she crossed Park Avenue and disappeared down 87th Street; until she returned home, around 10:30 p.m., I would be restless and agitated, unable to focus on anything or fall asleep. I would lie in my bed crying quietly, alone with my agonizing fear, imagining that something terrible would happen to her on her way home in the dark—a mugger would attack her, she would be taken from me, I would be left vulnerable and alone....

Although I had a vivid imagination, I never actually pictured what might happen to her. My fear was more centered on myself, on what would happen to me if she were to disappear and I was left on my own. Of course, I wouldn't really have been on my own; my brother and father would have been with me. But without my mother in the picture, I saw myself as bereft, abandoned and incapable of coping with life. And the more afraid I was of that scenario, the more obsessively I thought about it, as if I might prepare myself somehow for losing her by rehearsing it over and over in my waking nightmares.

It is a perfect Saturday in early October: the sky is a clear and brilliant blue through which the sunshine pours down on the fields and woodlands, setting the fall colors ablaze. Having just been released from my usual drab week in the city, I have been out roaming the countryside since dawn, admiring the hundreds of beautiful round spider webs strung up like fairy jewels in the deep dewy grass of the Lower Meadow; watching the swallows swooping and whirling in preparation for their long migration south; taking note with sadness of the appearance of the purple asters, the very last wildflowers to open before the frost turns everything brown. Coming up the path from the pond in the Lower Meadow, my canvas sneakers cold and wet with dew, I look up and am awe-struck at the sight of the old sugar maple tree on the hill, which I'd never really noticed before. Today it is resplendent, every leaf a fiery orange, its huge gnarled branches bending down nearly to the ground in an unmistakable gesture of benevolent grace, giving its blessing to the landscape below. For long moments I stand stock-still on the path, staring up at the tree and giving it my deepest, most focused attention, until I feel like I am merging with it, some of its slow, deep-rooted vitality mainlining right into my veins, its sugary orange glow lighting me from within. As I commune with the tree, a word surfaces in my mind: Yggdrasil.

I didn't get my first camera until I was about 12 years old. Before then, I used to take "memory pictures." I'd be in the midst of a moment or a scene that I wished could last forever, and I'd be determined to engrave it in my memory. I'd be still and quiet and focus intensely with all my senses on the scene I wanted to record, and I'd feel it imprinting itself upon my brain, indelibly. Even now, so many years later, I can clearly and easily call up many of the memory pictures I took in childhood, and I still give that tree a silent greeting of profound respect and love every time I pass it. Yggdrasil. I don't know how I knew about this mythic Norse tree of life as a child, but the name came to me with great surety that day, and it remains the name by which I call that noble old tree, one of the group of maple tree elders on that land whose roots mingle with my own, feeding my spirit as they watch over me through the years, always bringing me back to ground.

As a child, the old trees provided the conceptual bridge for me between the pre-colonial past of our property and my own time. In my early childhood, I absorbed the conventional narrative of the European "discovery" of the Americas: Christopher Columbus and Henry Hudson as heroes who gallantly sailed the ocean blue to lead the way into a grand new future for the poor persecuted Pilgrims. The uncivilized native people—the "Indians"—stood in awe of the Europeans, welcomed them and gave them gifts, and then faded away as the real work of settling the countryside began. Except that they didn't fade away for me. Even as a child, receiving the full force of the typical triumphalist colonial indoctrination, I remained curious about the Native peoples who had roamed the woods and fields before me. When I learned that the old maples on our property were at least 200 years old, and maybe quite a bit more, I realized that as young trees they might have witnessed the Native people I wanted so much to meet and know more about. I tried to imagine a young Mohican pausing under Yggdrasil, squatting with his back against the tree to eat a snack and gaze out over the landscape before picking up his bow and continuing on again. I kept my eyes on the ground on my early morning walks, looking for arrowheads he may have let fall.

It's a Saturday morning in the country, I'm eight years old, and my best friend Allison has just appeared, driven from her house up the hill by her parents. We are drawn together like magnet and metal, and go off into the sunny morning, leaving our parents talking around their coffee mugs. Without needing any cue, we follow our usual Saturday morning ritual, exchanging our journal notebooks to silently read what the other has written during the week. I have named my journal Tapestry, after the Carole King song, the first verse of which I inscribe at the beginning of each volume:

My life has been a tapestry of rich and royal hue
An ever-lasting vision, of the ever-changing view.
A wondrous woven magic, in bits of blue and gold
A tapestry to feel and see, impossible to hold.

Most of the time Allison and I don't discuss what we've read, but hug it to ourselves, the sharing of our secret interior life the sealing of our intimacy.

Done reading, we wander off into the sweet-smelling meadow, which is buzzing with bees attracted to the wild bee balm and tall stalks of goldenrod. "Let's play slave driver!" one of us says, and the other knows just what she has in mind. One of us will be the slave, the other the master; the master will drive the slave through the long grass, pretending that she's pulling a heavy load, and whipping her with a long stalk of mullein if she falters. We make our way over to the old hay wagons that are always parked in the far corner of the field, under the maple trees. "Get up there!" the master cries, and the slave complies, feeling fearful and powerless. Once up in the slatted wooden hay wagons, she cannot get down until the master gives permission. Or sometimes the game will shift, and the master will come up too, and now they will be refugees, fleeing their homeland in wagons, not knowing where they're bound, looking out bleakly into a landscape suddenly stark and unfamiliar.

Once my little brother, five years younger than Allison and me, tagged along, wanting to play with us. Slipping into our master and slave game, we made him the slave, and we giggled wickedly as we led him to the dark, cobwebby tool shed and locked him in it, snapping the bar down over the door so he couldn't open it from the inside. Furious and red-faced, he quickly climbed out of the grimy window, and he never asked to play with us again. I was shocked at his reaction—it was only a game! Just let's pretend! But even now, all these years later, he has not forgiven me.

When I turn nine, I am old enough to walk to school by myself, Mommy says. It is an easy walk from our apartment at 1060 Park Avenue, on the corner of 87th Street, to P.S. 6: past the dark brown stone Presbyterian Church, past the big Catholic Church set regally back from the street and up high, past several exclusive apartment buildings with their doormen standing watchfully inside the doors, turning finally onto 82nd Street, where the two-story red brick school takes up the entire block between 82nd and 81st streets along Madison Avenue, with the school yard on 82nd Street. The only tricky part of the route is at 86th Street and Park Avenue, a double-wide, busy intersection; but the affable old crossing guard, Marge, is always there to meet me, her electric blue eyes smiling out of her reddened, deeply lined face, shaded by the white pillbox cap that matches

her smart blue and white uniform. I enjoy the walk,
except for those few moments when Marge and I have
to wait by the bus stop on the northwest corner of
86th Street for the light to turn green, and the aged
city buses pull in to take on passengers. Enveloped in
huge clouds of hot, blue-white, foul-smelling exhaust,
I try to hold my breath but it's no use: I feel like I am
wilting to my core.

Those were some tough years in New York City.
My dad was mugged one night right on the corner
of Park Avenue and 87th street, walking our dachshund and within sight of the doorman—neither of
whom noticed anything amiss. Daddy was glad that
his young assailant, armed with a knife, did not
demand his whole wallet—he had been satisfied with
the offer of all the cash it contained. My brother was
mugged too, riding his bike in Central Park. Again,
it was a relief that the thieves were content to make
off with the bicycle, leaving my brother angry and
resentful but unharmed.

Sometimes on warm spring nights we would
take an after-dinner stroll up 87th street to Madison
Avenue and down Madison to Baskin-Robbins,
where it was a great treat to pick out some special
flavors for a double-decker sugar cone. My parents
would stroll along hand in hand, and we kids would
follow, in our own worlds. I loved to window-shop
along the avenue, attracted especially by the swanky
florist's window, crammed with lush orchids and

gladiolas and vivid African violets. If it was a nice night, we'd keep walking after we got our ice cream, going all the way down to 72nd Street on one side of Madison, and back up on the other, window-shopping all the way.

But for the most part, my brother and I didn't go out much after school. Sometimes we played in the dark hallway with the neighbor kids, running up and down the shiny red painted stairs, and slamming in and out of our adjoining apartments with their heavy iron fire doors and cryptic little peepholes. Most of the time we watched television after school, while my mom cooked dinner and we waited for Dad to come home from work. It seems to me that we watched endless episodes of *I Dream of Jeannie*, *Gilligan's Island* and *Hogan's Heroes*, waiting until we heard the door slam and then running out of the bedroom cheering, wrapping ourselves around our beaming father before he'd even had time to take his coat off.

My parents always had "cocktail time" before dinner. My father would leave work at 6 p.m. and was home punctually by 6:30, having ridden the IRT uptown from his office at 345 Park Avenue, down by the Pan Am Building. He'd take off his suit jacket and silk tie, change into his slippers and clink glasses with my mom, who always put out a nice spread of French or Italian cheeses, baguette or crackers, olives, celery, carrots and a double Scotch on the rocks.

"So, any good news or funny stories?" Dad would ask after he'd taken the edge off the day with a sip of his drink. My mother could usually oblige with some amusing stories about her interactions with the butcher, Ralph, or Madame Dumas, the doyenne of the bakery, or about one of her pottery classes at the 92nd Street Y. She grilled my dad about his gourmet lunches at some of the finest midtown restaurants. How had they cooked the calves' liver at the Brasserie? Those *pommes de terre* at Lutece, did they have garlic in them? You could see her taking mental notes, which she referred to as she pored over her growing collection of cookbooks and turned out dinner after dinner with the unstated aim of outdoing the chefs who pleased my father at lunchtime.

Guests who had the pleasure of joining us for a family meal would always gaze at my well-fed father in envy, saying, "You eat like this every day? Do you know how lucky you are?" Dad would nod, smiling at my mother, and say, "Yes, I've been trying to convince her to open a restaurant!" But my mom would shrug, not needing or wanting the pressure of going pro, content with turning out meal after perfect meal just for us, her little family. Tender double baby lamb chops in mustard butter, with parsley potatoes and string beans sautéed in garlic. Choucroute garni with pork and four kinds of German sausage, procured along with the sauerkraut from Bremen Haus on 86th Street, baked with fresh slab bacon, dry white wine, and whole peppercorns. Sizzling shrimp with black beans, stir-fried in her wok over the gas flame with garlic and ginger, served with sticky Chinese rice and stir-fried broccoli. Veal piccata made with the finest, melt-in-your-mouth veal cutlets, pounded extra-thin and sautéed quickly in olive oil, lemon, and capers. Chicken roasted whole with lemons, rosemary and garlic, on a bed of carrots, onions and potatoes. Every meal my mother made was saturated with loving, careful attention and I don't remember her ever having a dish go awry.

I want to create a Memory Box, a place to hold all my treasures and talismans. Mommy gives me a large shoebox and I cover it carefully with soft, fuzzy maroon contact paper, decorating the lid with a shiny silver moon and borders, also cut out of contact paper. I begin placing small objects in it, precious to me for various reasons. Inside the big box I keep the set of small colored Lucite boxes I had begged Mommy to buy me from Azuma, the Asian notions store on 86th Street. In one of these boxes I place a shiny green acorn, and in another, the gold and garnet ring my grandparents had given me for my birthday. In a small cube with drawers, covered in paper patterned with groovy 1970s orange and red swirls, I store the set of old coins Grandma had given me; in another drawer I keep the seashells and coral I collected from Cape Cod. The silver rattle with my initials engraved on it, a baby present, makes a musical, tinkling sound whenever I pick up the Memory Box to look through its contents.

I was always conscious of the passage of time. Sometimes that worked in my favor, as when I could tell myself with satisfaction that it was already Wednesday, the turning point of the week—only two more days to go until we were off to the country! But the weekends were always so short, and there was nothing I could do to slow the precious country time down.

On the last day of summer, I am out doing what my parents call "moaming"—a combination of roaming around and moaning, grieving that I will soon be torn from the countryside I love. As soon as the goldenrod starts to show up in August, I feel the first pricks of sadness, and begin obsessively trying to get the most out of every remaining day of our stay in the country—rising early to catch the sunrise, staying outside as long as possible, all day and into the long, slow twilights to watch the stars come out and the fireflies flicker. But eventually, no matter how much I try to hold it off, the day comes when we must pack up and leave.

"We'll be back next Friday," Mommy says compassionately. I nod miserably. I don't want to leave; don't want to begin again the weekly shuttle back and forth between city and country, when every Sunday afternoon involves emptying out the

refrigerator, packing up the suitcases and folding our-selves into the car for the two-hour ride that will take us from the green rolling hills of the country to the dirty, smelly concrete of Manhattan. I cry silently as we swing onto the highway, and I'm still sniffling as we exit the West Side Highway at 96th street, electric door locks snapping shut as we make our way across town, past hot, sweaty families hanging out on their stoops, young men drinking from brown bagged bottles, older men panhandling and wiping windshields at the stoplights, children laughing and chasing each other through fire hydrants opened to spray water violently into the street. Seen through the sealed comfort of Daddy's air-conditioned Peugeot, it's like passing through an entirely different world. I close my eyes, leaning my head on the glass, sending my spirit back to the green hillside I will haunt in memory for the coming week.

My whole childhood moved between the poles of city and country, rhythmically, like a pendu-lum swinging back and forth, held securely by my strong attachment to my parents. I did not push the boundaries they set for me. I did not feel any inclination to challenge their rules, which were few enough and mostly unspoken: be respectful of others, be responsible, don't do anything dan-gerous, work hard at school and help out around the house as needed. One of the few actual prohi-bitions laid on me in my childhood was to never,

ever go north of 96th Street, the great dividing line between the clean, calm Upper East Side, and the dirty, gritty streets of East Harlem. My parents were not racist, but they were cautious, and in the 1960s and 70s when I was growing up, New York City was full of danger, with most of the threat seeming to come from the Black community. As a child I saw nothing of the big picture of how and why this violence had come to be; I understood only that I should cross the street in a hurry if I saw a group of Black teenage boys coming my way; that I should always use Park Avenue as my north-south avenue, so as to rely on the protection of the (always white, mostly Irish) doormen; and that I should never be out alone after dark.

Three Memories from my 10th year

It's Saint Patrick's Day, and as Mommy hurries us home from school we see something I've never seen before: big, rowdy white men clutching brown-paper-wrapped cans and bottles, shouting and swearing right on the quiet streets of the Upper East Side. 86th Street is blocked off with blue police barricades that we have to cross on our route from P.S. 6 to our home at 1060 Park. I want to go to see the parade, but Mommy says no, my brother and I can watch from our 9th floor window. So we do, sitting on the radiator by the one window in the apartment with a narrow view of 86th

Street. We can see phalanxes of marching bands and floats going by, and hear the lively marching music. All of a sudden, we see something else: a police officer on horseback, galloping along Park Avenue chasing a man who is running away, shouting loudly. As we watch, horrified, the police officer slams his stick down on the man's head and shoulders, and he falls to his knees. I am too shocked and afraid to watch any more.

It's a rare weekend when we are in the city because Mommy and Daddy had to go to an office party on Saturday night. On Sunday afternoon, as a special treat, we are going to the movies! We walk over to the big movie theater on 86th Street, which is crowded with a long line of people waiting to buy tickets, cordoned off from the ticket-holders, who are also waiting to get into the theater. Daddy buys the tickets and hands them to Mommy, and then takes off into the theater looking for the bathroom. We wait on the line. A few minutes later, I am shocked to see Daddy being hauled out of the theater by the scruff of his jacket by the tallest Black man I have ever seen. Daddy is thrashing and trying to turn around to talk to the guard. Mommy rushes forward, waving her tickets in his face: "We have tickets!" she cries. "He was just using the rest room!" The guard deposits Daddy with us and stares down at Mommy dispassionately. "No one is allowed in the theater until we

open the gate," he says tonelessly, and disappears.
Daddy is red-faced and furious.

"Shall we go?" Mommy says anxiously. "Let's just
go." But we have bought tickets. We stay. All through
the movie, I am aware of Daddy in the seat next to
me, fuming and angry. The only other time I've seen
him this angry is once when we were leaving the city
on the East Side Drive and another driver, moving
aggressively to pass us on the ramp to the highway,
scraped up against our car. Both men stopped and
got out of their cars, Daddy looking small next to
the big Black man who faced him aggressively. "The
hell with it!" Daddy said, and got back into the car.
He fumed all the way to the highway, just like he's
fuming now at the movie theater. He doesn't like to
be disrespected.

Mommy has just turned out the lights in the room
I share with my brother. It is snowing outside, the
whirling snow clearly visible in the pink glow of the
streetlights. Suddenly I hear something banging and
tapping on the window. "Danny! Do you hear that?"
I whisper to my brother, who sits up, peering sleepily at the window. "Mommy!" I call. "Something's
at the window!" Mommy comes back, prepared to
tell us soothingly that nothing is there. But something is there. It's a bird, flapping madly at the
window, and when Mommy opens it the bird flies in
with a rush of cold air and snowflakes. It's a blue
parakeet, half-frozen and so relieved to have found

shelter from the storm. Of course we will adopt her.
We name her Bluebell.

In fourth grade, my nice young teacher, Mrs.
Appel, went on maternity leave after Thanksgiving.
Mr. Krugman replaced her—a heavyset, gray-haired,
solemn man who had little to offer besides discipline. I quickly learned that he didn't mind if
I spent the day reading under my desk, and so as
the year plodded along, I kept my eyes glued to the
pages of the book in my lap. That spring I discovered
The Hobbit and the *Lord of the Rings* trilogy, quite by
accident in the public library, and I devoured them
with the sense of being guided through an entirely
new world by a mind who understood my hunger
for adventure, magic and wonder. The drone of Mr.
Krugman and the harsh fluorescent lights of the
classroom faded into the background as I followed
the elves through a forest of silver-barked, gold-
en-leaved trees and accompanied Frodo on his trek to
Mordor for the very first time. The contrast between
the lush, vibrant landscape of the Ent-forests or the
Elven glades and the dead, blasted wastes of Mordor
echoed my own experience of going back and forth
between the verdant landscape of the country and
the dry concrete canyons of Manhattan. I knew
which side I was on.

A sun washed morning in early spring. I grab a slice
of dark, raisin-studded pumpernickel bread, slather

it with fluffy cream cheese from the orange and white Zabar's container, and head joyfully out into the fresh air. All around me the little maple leaves are just budding, bright green and vibrating with vitality. The phoebes are busy building their woven grass nest on our front door light, and the swallows that craft their mud pockets under the overhang on the south side of the house dive-bomb me aggressively as I step out the door, protecting their territory. Relishing the rich, chewy bread and cream cheese, I saunter down the driveway, heading on out on my usual morning walk: up the dirt road a ways, then across the woodland stream and up the mountain to the ridge top where I like to sit in a clearing under a sun-warmed pine tree and wait to see if a deer will pass by.

On this day, though, I am brought to a sudden halt by a shocking sight at the bottom of our driveway: the power company has come during the week while we were away and cut down a big swath of young trees underneath the wires, leaving behind heaps of dying limbs and saplings, heavy with oozing sap and shriveling new leaves. Seized by a gut-wrenching feeling of horror, I am suddenly crying, crooning to the trees, overwhelmed with a feeling of shame and guilt—why are my people, humans, so destructive, so wanton, so careless and thoughtless?

I run back up the driveway to tell Mommy and Daddy, and am surprised and upset at their resigned response: they shrug and shake their heads—there is *nothing to be done about it, they tell me. Turning away from them, I feel my initial sorrow and shock give way to hot anger. I grab my notebook and pen and head back out to the woods, this time to my special spot: a circle of moss-covered rocks high on a ledge, carpeted by fine wood grass and surrounded by small trees. I begin to write furiously.*

Out of this anguished furor came my first serious piece of writing: the story of Estrella, a tree nymph who joins forces with a group of animals who are worried and upset because the humans are cutting down their forest. Estrella and a few of the animals decide to set out on a quest to find a solution to the destruction. But the story trailed off as they began their journey, because I couldn't imagine who might be capable of stopping the destruction. I couldn't imagine a solution. I believed in forest spirits, but I did not believe in God, in an all-powerful being who might be able to intercede in the doings of human beings; and I knew, from reading *Ranger Rick*, *National Wildlife* and *International Wildlife*, that although some humans tried to stop the tide of destruction, it was relentless. Reading these magazines opened up a much bigger world for me—I learned of the slaughter of elephants for their tusks, of the ever-shrinking habitat of the Siberian tigers, of the way people waited on the beach to steal sea turtle eggs as fast as they were laid—but it also made me feel dispiritingly powerless.

During this time in my life I prayed often. The being to whom I directed my prayers was a serene, benevolent tiger I called Majesty, whose photograph I'd taped up on the wall above my bed, and into whose golden eyes I often stared as I whispered prayers and confidences. I believed in the spiritual power of Majesty, but I had no illusions about his being powerful enough to stop big men with bulldozers and chain saws.

All spring we have been rehearsing for the last play we will be putting on as a class at P.S. 6: Fiddler on the Roof. In fourth grade we did You're a Good Man, Charlie Brown and in fifth grade, The Wizard of Oz, in both cases doing what we thought, and our parents and teachers agreed, was an excellent job. I had tried out for Dorothy in fifth grade, but of course Janine, who took acting and singing classes, had been chosen. In "Fiddler," I am given the role of the narrator. Since the play has been abridged, there are long chunks of narration between each scene, which I am expected to memorize and recite. I practice my lines feverishly, repeating them over and over during the long car rides upstate and back that spring. But now the moment of truth has arrived, I'm standing on the darkened stage with a bright spotlight on me, in front of a packed auditorium of parents, teachers and schoolmates, and—and—

I cannot remember my lines. I am absolutely blank. Panic, fear, shame, disappointment....until finally the teacher whispers the first line to me and my brain begins to function again.

I knew the story of *Fiddler on the Roof* perfectly, but when I had to recite it word for word from memory, in words not my own, the terror of getting it wrong was entirely paralyzing. How different this was from the imaginative theater I played every weekend with Allison out in the fields and woods, joyfully taking on roles and making up dialogue with grace and intensity. From that time on, I never again participated in a school play, and the very idea of public speaking would set me hyperventilating with anxiety. For this, I have my sixth grade teacher, Miss Keegan, to thank. A tall, skinny, humorless woman, she was very different from my hip, fun-loving fifth grade teacher, Ms. Mosson, who wore tight jeans, suede vests with fringes and cowboy boots to school, and cheered us on energetically from behind her big mod tinted glasses. Miss Keegan was pale, severe and serious; I could easily imagine her in the wimple and habit that must have been her uniform before she gave up her career as a nun to come teach at P.S. 6. She wore high-collared shirts, plain navy blue skirts, and dull black pumps every day, and she seemed to be in a constant state of low-grade irritation that could erupt into outright rage at the slightest provocation.

With such a teacher, talking to Paul in class was risky; but worth the risk to me, because I had such a crush on him. I was in love with his big brown eyes and long, wispy blond hair that fell artfully over his forehead, hanging down loosely over his bony shoulders. He was always being sought after by the coolest, most attractive girls in the class, Deirdre and Emily, who seemed to exert some kind of magnetic pull on the available handful of handsome boys. I, hopelessly uncool though very smart, was not invited to join their crowd. But in sixth grade I was lucky enough to have been assigned to sit just behind Paul, and it pleased me that he would frequently twist around in his seat to consult with me on schoolwork. It also pleased me to see Emily throw dirty looks over her shoulder at Paul from her assigned seat in the very front row, right in front of the ever-scowling Miss Keegan.

I never got in trouble for talking with Paul, but Miss Keegan did get furious at me and my friend Kim when she caught us in a lie. It had something to do with library books—returning them late, or not checking them out properly. She flew into a towering rage, wrote angry letters home to our parents, spoke to the principal about us, and made us feel thoroughly guilty. Kim and I knew she was overreacting, and that our mothers would not be angry at the small sin we had committed with the library books. No harm had been done in the end, after all. But for Miss Keegan, we were forever tarnished by our descent into *lying*. There was no redemption.

For weeks now, when Allison's parents arrive on Saturday mornings for coffee, their conversation with my parents, especially Daddy, has been louder and more animated than I've ever heard it. As Allison and I slip away to exchange our journals as usual, I hear unfamiliar words and terms that arouse my curiosity: gas shortage, Watergate, impeachment, indictment...

I don't understand it. I only know that the adults in my life are agitated and angry; that Mommy has started watching TV during the day, which she NEVER does, tuning in to what seem to me to be endlessly boring episodes of a program called The Hearings; and that Daddy has started meeting with his old friend Alan Chartock on Saturday afternoons, to work on a book called How to Impeach a President. They sit together at the picnic table under the big maple tree, poring intently over yellow legal pads on which they've scribbled in barely legible pencil.

The excitement of it intrigues me, but it doesn't seem to be any of my concern. I'm more interested in going for my walks up the mountain, or getting Mommy to take me for a horseback riding lesson. Horses have become my passion, and I am jealous of my friend Allison, who has what I want more than anything in the world: she lives year-round in the country, and she has not only one, but two horses of her own. Never mind that Charlie and Coco are old and swaybacked; never mind that Charlie is lazy, while Coco has a fierce temper and a tendency to shy at nothing. Allison can go down to the pasture after school and pet them, brush them and ride them to her heart's content, something that I, chained to my life in the city, can never have.

One Saturday morning in May we put bridles on Charlie and Coco and take them out bareback, walking down the quiet dirt road to the long narrow field that Allison's parents inexplicably call "the Television House Field." Once out in the short, stubbly grass, we kick and coax the two horses into a trot, and soon, intoxicated by their own speed, they break into a canter and then a full-out, rollicking gallop. I bend low over Charlie's mane, digging in to his broad ribcage with my knees, feeling the wind blowing through my hair as he gallops at what seems like a breakneck pace. Dimly, in the back of my mind, I'm worried that he might step into a woodchuck hole and stumble or get hurt, but this caution is nothing compared to the thrill of the madcap run down the long field, with Allison on Coco right next to me. It is a moment I wish could go on forever. In my memory, it does.

I was totally crazy for horses from the age of about 10 to 14. I had a full set of Breyer model horses, for which I fashioned elaborate saddles and bridles, using soft chamois cloth, leather lacing and brass wire. I had every book of horse stories available, and big, lavishly illustrated reference books about horses as well. In 1973, when I was 10,

Secretariat won the Triple Crown, and I watched every race, doting on the big red stallion as if I were his mother—or his owner. I created a detailed scrapbook of his career, carefully cutting articles out of my father's *New York Times*, including the color pictures from the Sunday Magazine. And whenever I could, I rode: lessons on summer weekday afternoons, two blessed weeks of horseback riding day camp, and all the riding time on old Charlie and Coco that I could sneak in. I yearned to have my own horse...which I imagined as a pet that would follow me everywhere, just like the horses in my favorite books, *Misty of Chincoteague, Black Gold* or *My Friend Flicka.* I had it all figured out: we would fence in the Lower Meadow, which had plenty of grass and a small pond right in it. We'd built a little barn for shelter, and our neighbor Jack would be in charge of feeding the horse while we were in the city during the weeks.

But my parents did not agree, and it seemed that no amount of begging, pleading, wheedling or cajoling could persuade them. It was simply out of the question.

I am hanging around in the kitchen watching Mommy cook dinner, feeling very excited and pleased because I've just received some good news: I got into Hunter! I don't really know what Hunter is all about, but I know it's a much better alternative than going to Wagner, the local public junior high school. Daddy comes home and I rush over to tell him, receiving a big hug and something unusual: he has a present for me! I can't remember him ever picking out a present for me—that's always Mommy's department. I open it with excitement, and find a fat, gleaming red enameled pen, trimmed with gold. "Congratulations!" Daddy says, grinning at me. The knowledge that he's proud of me makes me so happy I am speechless, both embarrassed and delighted. I will treasure that pen for years to come.

When I started Hunter College High School, in the 7th grade, it was located on two beat-up floors of an office building between 45th and 46th streets on Lexington Avenue. We kids would get into the elevator with the business men in their suits and the secretaries in their heels; as they got off we were treated to glimpses of the polished chrome, thick carpets and elegant lighting of their offices. Our two floors always felt cramped, with kids jostling and hurrying to get from class to class through narrow, shabby halls with dull fluorescent lighting.

The year I entered Hunter was the first year boys were admitted, and there were something like eight boys among the 400 girls in my class. We never saw them, and I didn't care. I was totally focused on my classes. I loved my two Spanish teachers: the first a tiny, dowdy woman with an impeccable Peninsular accent, who liked to show us posters and tell us about all the many places she had visited in Spain; and the second a beautiful Cuban woman who was young, high-powered and got me speaking Spanish fast. I loved my English teachers too: Mr. McNeil, who I recognized as gay before I even knew such an identity existed, and Mrs. Robinson, a tall, strikingly beautiful and smart African American woman. Both ran lively discussion classes that provoked us students to think more deeply about books and stories than I had imagined possible.

The big house across the road, the seat of the old Easterbrook estate, is now owned by a couple from New York who are rarely in residence. They have constructed a kennel outside, and they leave two dogs there all winter, a charismatic Samoyed named Tolstoy, and a big, phlegmatic Irish Wolfhound, Guinness. Our farmer neighbor Jack comes in daily to feed them, but otherwise they're on their own in the outdoor kennel, day in and day out. I am horrified that anyone would treat such delightful dogs in this callous, unfeeling manner, and I spend all my time there during the Christmas holiday, keeping the dogs company, petting them as best I can through the squares of the chain-link fence. Tolstoy frequently escapes and takes off, and often giant Guinness shows up by himself at our house, looking for companionship. I take his big, almost horse-sized head in my arms and love him with all my heart. If I can't have a horse, at least I must have a dog.

Our Dachshund Inchy died of kidney failure when I was about 10, and after that I began an intensive campaign to get a dog of my own. My mom had already adopted Tigger, a stray who became a one-person cat, totally fixated on my mother. I desperately wanted a dog who would be entirely devoted to me. When simply asking did not work, I began wheedling and cajoling. When that didn't work, I began pleading. And when pleading didn't work, I got angry and started what my parents called "the silent treatment." I refused to speak to them or even make eye contact. I moped conspicuously. I wanted a dog. I wanted a dog. I wanted a dog.

The silent treatment eventually worked. When I was thirteen, my parents were finally persuaded to let me have a dog—a Samoyed like Tolstoy, who had eventually been taken in by Allison's family. I pored over the Dogs for Sale ads in *The New York Times*, and found a listing for a new litter of show-quality Samoyed puppies in New Jersey. I was so excited when my mom and I called to find out about them, and beside myself with joy when we drove out there one weekend to meet MY PUPPY, who I'd decided to name Pushkin. He was the biggest one of the litter, and lay calmly in the center of his much more active brothers and sisters, who were frisking about in the playpen when we arrived. Since he was destined for an apartment, the breeder thought the calmest dog would be the

best for us. I stroked his soft white fur, admired his
little black button eyes and nose, and was thrilled
when he was lifted out of the playpen and placed
on my lap. Pushkin, my baby!

We had to wait until he was old enough to be
separated from his mother, and in that month of
waiting we took a family trip out West, landing in
Jackson Hole, Wyoming, and driving through the
Tetons and up through Montana to Lake Louise,
Glacier National Park, and on to Calgary to fly
home. It was the most extraordinary landscape I'd
ever seen: so big, so open, so majestic—so unlike the
crowded streets of Manhattan, or the tight, sheltered
hills and valleys of upstate New York. The air was
cold and crisp, even in June, and the fields of bright,
sturdy wildflowers were tinged with light snow in the
mornings. I loved every moment of that trip. It was
to be the last one I'd take with my family for many
years, at least if a plane was necessary, because once
I became Pushkin's mother I absolutely refused to
leave him—not with any of my mom's friends, and
certainly not in a kennel.

*We've just gotten home from our trip out West, and
tomorrow we're going to pick up my puppy from the
breeder. But it's the Fourth of July, 1976, and we're
going over to Mimi and Hal's Riverside Drive apartment to watch the special Bicentennial Tall Ships
parade on the Hudson. Their luxurious apartment
has huge plate glass windows overlooking the river,*

and it's festive with food, drink and people. I find a place by a window and am entranced by the slow, stately procession of the great ships of sail from many different countries, including replicas of the original tall ships that came over from Europe in the colonial days. Later in the evening, the fireworks begin, and the display is spectacular. But all I can think about, really, is this: Tomorrow I'm getting MY DOG!!!

Pushkin was my baby and my beloved, my protector and my best friend in those awkward middle school years. He grew into a big, headstrong, lively dog who loved nothing more than to pull me down the avenues and into Central Park. Finally I was able to go walking in the city by myself, as I had been doing for years in the country. Pushkin and I would take long walks, window-shopping down Madison Avenue, coming back along the leafy cobblestoned sidewalk on Fifth Avenue by the park. With him prancing at my side, I could even venture into the park, which had been entirely off limits unless accompanied by my parents. Pushkin and I explored the Ramble behind Belvedere Castle, walked around the Reservoir and along the bridle path, and went all the way down to the 72nd Street Boat Basin to watch the men and boys skillfully piloting their remote-control sailboats from one end of the pond to the other.

All that came later, of course, once he grew up. When we picked him up on July 5th, we brought him straight to the country, where he was house-broken and learned his first great trick—to "stay" on command. By the time we got back to the city that fall, he was a gangly adolescent, and I wanted to take him to obedience class, to teach him to heel and come when called. The only class my mom could find was all the way down on 57th Street and First Avenue. My mom was doubtful because it was so far from our apartment, but I insisted that Pushkin and I could walk there. So we did. We walked all the way from Park Avenue at 87th Street to 57th Street and First Avenue, took our chaotic hour-long lesson with a dozen dogs of all sizes and shapes crammed into a dark little room in an old, grimy building, and then walked back uptown again as the streetlights along Park Avenue began to wink on in the dusk.

The class lasted six weeks, and we attended faithfully. But Pushkin never did learn to heel or come when he was called. A Samoyed is a pulling dog, and he continued to pull me down the streets, despite the nylon choke collar around his neck. I didn't really mind. The important thing was that I felt safe with him by my side. He was a loyal family dog and not that interested in other people, who admired his handsome, show-dog frame and fluffy, snow-white coat, but mostly gave him a wide berth as we made our way down the streets of Manhattan. Once, on a crowded Lexington Avenue sidewalk, he lunged unexpectedly, growling at an approaching man, who snarled back and pulled out a knife that he waved menacingly at both of us. I pulled Pushkin away and kept going, scared but proud, too, that he'd sensed the hidden menace in that man.

My dad has made partner at his law firm, and it has been decided that my parents will sell their apartment at 1060 Park and move somewhere bigger. For a few weekends, instead of going upstate, we've gone out to Westchester to look at possible houses with a realtor. Driving around Scarsdale, Larchmont and nearby Greenwich, Connecticut, I am delighted by all the trees and green, open spaces. I want to move here, to get out of the city! It would even be worth the terror of changing schools. We look at several houses, each one, it seems, larger and grander than the last. My favorite is a huge Tudor house in Larchmont, all stone, stucco, wood and slate roof tiles, set in a manicured, roomy garden. The house has separate kids' quarters on the second floor, a huge game room, and an intercom in every room. When we get back home to 1060 Park that afternoon, I get out my Magic Markers and drawing pad and, in my little maid's room off the kitchen, busy myself drawing the imposing front of the Larchmont house, and the floor plan as well as I can remember it. I beg Mommy and Daddy to buy it so we can live there, the next best thing to the country!

But they have other ideas. One night after my dad gets home from work, we walk up Park Avenue to 93rd Street, where the realtor meets us and leads us into a cool, shady courtyard with a big fountain splashing amid a garden of small trees, shrubs and flowers. We ride up the wood paneled elevator and I'm surprised when the door opens on a landing with only one door—I am used to the dark, fluorescent-lit hallway of 1060, which has four apartments per floor. This is a large, imposing door with a gold handle and fancy molding on it. I am already impressed. We go in and the sense of space and light is astounding: beyond the entryway, which has curved walls, museum-like recessed lighting, and doors leading off it in all directions, there is a huge living room with windows on the far end, apparently overlooking a balcony, since I can see the tops of trees through the glass, even though we're on the 11th floor.

As the adults talk, I walk into the living room, wanting to go and see more of the greenery outside the windows. I glance around me, taking in the polished parquet wood floors, a small black marble fireplace with an elaborately carved wooden mantle, ornate stiff-looking chairs and couches, and a series of huge fine art prints on one wall, depicting...Nazis in spiked metal helmets and full uniform, with angry, snarling faces, stabbing downwards with bayonets! I shrink away in horror and speed back to my mother's side, tapping her arm and gesturing wordlessly at the prints, which I now see spill out into the entryway as well. She shakes her head at me, meaning 'We're not going to talk about that now,' and we continue our *tour of the sprawling apartment, with its big dining room and den in addition to the vast living room, three enormous bedrooms, three marbled bathrooms, a huge butler's pantry and eat-in kitchen, and a small, dark warren of maid's quarters in the back, complete with their own bathroom. I don't know it that night, but this is the place I will be calling home for the next twenty years.*

Later my parents learned that the apartment had been sub-let to a branch of the infamous Von Ribbentrop family, who were obviously not afraid to display their Nazi sympathies in the privacy of their home. My family, who would have been on the receiving end of those razor-sharp bayonets back in Europe, laughed nervously whenever we remembered those evil-looking prints. We never talked about the Holocaust.

When we moved into Apartment 11G at 1185 Park Avenue, all of our furniture and boxes from 1060 Park fit into one corner of the huge living room. My mother got busy with her eccentric Chinese decorator friend and began several years of busy renovating, painting, tiling and the installation of gleaming new bookshelves, display cases and cabinets; forays to lighting, kitchen, bath and furniture showrooms; exciting trips to the auction at Sotheby's; and endless framing of paintings and prints, many by my mom's artist friends. Eventually the parade of workmen slowed to a trickle. The

rooms were all handsomely painted in deep, dramatic colors, elegantly furnished and properly lit with
chandeliers and spot fixtures; the kitchen and long
pantry were freshly painted and tiled, and the walls
in the servants' quarters were removed, transforming the dark warren into a big, brightly lit pottery
studio for my mom and her friend Mimi, complete
with two electric wheels, a slab roller, a big plaster
wedging board and an electric kiln so big that my
mom had to stand on a stool to stack the bottom
shelves. The back elevator men and Tom, the burly
Irish back gate security guard, got used to the sight
of my mother running out in her clay-spattered
jeans and tee shirts, her wire grocery cart in tow, to
grab some lamb chops for dinner, along with some
vegetables at the Korean market, and a baguette and
apple tarts at Dumas. On the days when she had
a thousand pounds of stoneware delivered, along
with another five hundred pounds of porcelain,
Tom grinned extra wide, as she always gave the back
door staff a good tip for carrying it all up to the
studio on the ware-trucks. She was not the typical
1185 Park Avenue matron.

*In the summer of my fourteenth year, my parents have
an important office party to attend, and so we do
something unprecedented; we reverse direction and go
into Manhattan on a hot Wednesday afternoon in
July. Allison comes with us, the trip to the city a treat
for her. My brother is away, visiting our grandparents*

in Florida. We go through our usual Sunday after-noon routine of stopping by the garage on 93rd and Second Avenue first, to pick up the attendant who will ride up to 1185 with us, wait while we unpack the car in the courtyard, and bring the car back down to the garage. It's blazingly bright and humid, the kind of sticky day that makes me want to head for the pond, or go stick my feet in the cold rushing waters of the stream. But here we are in the city. We close all the windows and crank up the air conditioners; there is one in each room of the apartment, and in a couple of hours they have the whole place nice and cool. My parents get into their gala finery and head out, leaving Allison and me to watch TV with Pushkin at our feet.

We're halfway through a TV movie, sitting bored through the endless commercials, when suddenly the screen goes dead and we find ourselves sitting in the dim light of the twilight outside the windows. It is eerily quiet at first, and then there are shouts and whistles from outside. Something has happened; the power is out. Allison and I look at each other, not knowing what to do. We go into the kitchen, which has a view out over the East River, towards Queens and the big airports. The cityscape, usually twinkling with lights, is totally dark. This is much bigger than just our building.

I'm worried about my parents, out there in the dark; but since Allison is with me, I try to keep my panic under control. Eventually they come huffing and puffing up the back stairs and drag themselves *into the kitchen to tell us about how they had to walk all the way uptown through the dark streets. By the time we all go to bed, there are sounds of smashing glass and raucous voices coming up from Lexington Avenue. We know we're safe, with our security guards manning the big locked gates of 1185. I fall asleep expecting the power to be back on when we wake up.*

But the power did not go back on the next morning. It was another hot, humid day, this time with no air conditioning, no refrigeration, and no running water. We couldn't just get in our car and head back to the country, because it was buried in a subterranean garage, accessible only by electric elevator. Pushkin, Allison and I made several laborious trips down the 11 flights of stairs and back up again with plastic buckets of water from the courtyard fountain, so at least we'd be able to flush the toilet as needed, and Pushkin could have a drink. Without TV or radio it was hard to know what was going on, but we gathered from talking with the building staff that the whole city was without power, and that there had been serious looting during the night.

In the afternoon, we all took a walk over to Central Park, where it seemed that half of Manhattan was out strolling, trying to stay cool. Hours went by. Around dinnertime the familiar green lights on the Triboro Bridge winked on cheerfully, along with glimmering lights all over Queens; but we were still in the dark. Finally, around 9 p.m., the lights on the Upper East Side came on and cheers resounded through the concrete canyons, an expression of our collective sense of relief as the refrigerators started to hum again and we could close the windows against the humid night air and fire up the air conditioners. Twenty-five hours without power felt like a very long time, especially in the city where so much of life depended on it. This was one of the few instances in my early life where the sense of limitless abundance came screeching to a halt.

As we move into the teenage years, something happens to my friendship with Allison. She is closing off from me, turning away. She doesn't want to exchange journal notebooks anymore, and we suddenly have little to say to each other. She is very involved with her boyfriend—a much older man she met working at a restaurant. I don't have a boyfriend. She spends a lot of time going for runs—long, arduous runs on the hilly dirt roads around her house at the top of the mountain. And she doesn't seem to eat. She gets thinner and thinner, until it's painful to see the way her collarbones jut out from her shoulders. Her once swelling, buxom breasts get small and pointy, and the flesh seems to melt away from her hips, until she looks like a narrow teenage boy, with over-developed calf and thigh muscles. I am bewildered by these changes in her, sad and hurt that she no longer seems to care about maintaining our old intimacy. It's a loss I can scarcely begin to measure.

Eventually my mother put a name to what was happening with Allison: anorexia. We had a book about the stages of adolescence, and I looked up anorexia anxiously, wanting to understand. According to the book, it was all about rebellion and anger, turned inward rather than outward—which is why it was more common in girls than in boys. It made sense to me, given what I knew of Allison's home life. But understanding didn't make it easier for me to lose my best friend, or to watch as she plunged into struggles for which we had no words. I couldn't help her; she made it clear that she didn't need or want my companionship. So I left her alone.

I too was self-conscious about my weight, the hissing insult "Fatso" still echoing in my ears. I began jogging with Pushkin around the Reservoir in Central Park in the city, and up the road in the country. In 8th and 9th grade, I went through a period of trying to cut down on eating, taking only a few carrot sticks and a yogurt for my school lunch, and avoiding bread and desserts. But I never had the iron willpower and discipline that Allison displayed. I jogged in a leisurely way, giving up as soon as I felt shin splints coming on, and I never stopped eating my mother's fabulous dinners. Being thin, desirable as it might be, just wasn't that important to me.

I am rushing down the crowded subway steps at 46th street/Grand Central after school, heading for the uptown IRT train. A bunch of people are coming up the steps as I go down. I pay no attention, focused on my own destination and using my New York-style peripheral vision so as to avoid any eye contact. All of a sudden I feel a stabbing pain on my chest. On my breast! I stop, gasping, not sure what has happened, and look behind me up the steps. No one seems to have noticed anything. Everyone is running up and down the steps the way they always do. It takes me a few beats to realize that some man has just pinched my breast, hard! I feel angry and violated and a little scared. My breasts are new to me; I do not wear a bra. I am wearing a sleeveless shirt, and yes, they must bounce as I jog down the subway stairs. I never thought about it before. I will have to think about it now.

In the fall of 1977, Hunter High School moved into its new building, the renovated Park Avenue Armory between 94th and 95th Streets—right across from 1185. After three years of commuting to school via public transportation, I could now just hop across the street to class, and come home whenever I had a free period. I loved to eat lunch at home with my mother and her studio partner Mimi. They would work in the studio all morning, and then come into the big bright kitchen in their clay-spattered aprons, competing with each other to see who had the more savory leftovers to pull out for lunch. I found their conversation much more interesting than anything I imagined my school friends might have been talking about. After school, I'd take Pushkin on long walks down Fifth Avenue and back up Madison, window-shopping; or I'd sit on the floor in my bedroom with the door closed, guitar cradled in my arms, playing through my whole repertoire of my father's folksongs. Sometimes I'd play in front of the mirror, staring at myself as I sang the sad, romantic ballads and wondering if I would ever have the courage to sing these songs for friends—if that is, I could ever find friends I might feel like singing for.

That was the year I started baking, working my way through the Maida Heatter cookbooks, each recipe more buttery and luscious than the last. I'd set up my mother's big KitchenAid mixer on the white marble counter and work with total concentration to sift the flour, cream the butter, add the eggs one by one, then the vanilla and sugar, and finally the milk and flour in alternating additions until the batter was ready to pour into the buttered and floured pan. Many things in life were beyond my control, but not baking—by following Maida Heatter's directions closely, with a little guidance from my mother, I could almost always get it right.

On a warm spring night, I'm coming back home from walking Pushkin over to Central Park. As usual, after I come through the big vaulted gateway to 1185, I stop at the office to talk with Gino, pulling Pushkin in behind me. Gino looks up from his seat at the

desk, next to the old-fashioned switchboard, and his
face brightens to see me. He is pale and thin, with big
soft brown eyes, and a wide expressive mouth. I first
started talking with him when he was working as the
elevator man in the G-H apartment line, his job to
push the buttons for us in the evening hours, between
4 and 11 p.m. Riding the elevator night after night,
we started talking about Pushkin and our friend-
ship proceeded from there. He's the youngest of all
the 1185 staff, but older than me—I don't know how
much older, maybe he's 20? He lives downtown in an
apartment in the East Village, and he's told me how
he grew in a Catholic orphanage on Long Island. It
sounds like something right out of Dickens to me,
and increases my interest in him. I know the other
building staff think it's strange that I spend so much
time talking with Gino, but I don't care. Nothing
else matches the thrill I get when his smiling eyes lock
on mine.

Once I invited Gino up for lunch in our apartment. I knew I was doing something a little risqué,
but my mom didn't seem to mind. I made sure to
make the date on a day when I knew she'd be out, so
we'd have the kitchen to ourselves. I felt very grown
up, making him a fresh pot of coffee and serving
ham sandwiches on baguette. He seemed nervous,
and glad enough to disappear back into the bowels
of the building when his lunch break was over. A
few days later, Gino told me that I'd have to stop

coming by the office, because he'd been told that if he didn't stop hanging out with me, he'd be fired. Seeing my crestfallen face, he suggested that we take our dogs for a walk together, away from 1185.

So one Friday afternoon we met at the 91st Street entrance to Central Park, he hopping out of a cab with his brown and white springer spaniel at his side, me strolling up with Pushkin straining to check out this new dog friend. It was May and the magnolias and cherry trees in the park were in full bloom. It felt like a dream, walking through the paths strewn with pink blossoms, talking easily with my tall, handsome friend Gino as our dogs romped ahead of us. We sat on the rocks by the reservoir and talked and talked until it was time for me to go home for dinner. It was a magical afternoon.

Before I knew it, it was summer, and I was back in the country. This time I would not be going back to the city at the end of the summer—I'd be going to college in the fall. I was excited, but sad to leave Gino behind, and I wrote him several letters at the beginning of the summer, waiting impatiently for his reply. When it came, it was not what I expected. It was a long letter, written in his distinctive block letter style on yellow lined notepaper. In it, Gino told me that he was gay, and had a boyfriend. He hoped we could still be friends. I put the letter away in my Memory Box, alongside the scribbled note from my sixth grade crush, Paul, and the acorn, garnet ring and silver coins, and turned my face to

the future: a three-week bike trip through Vermont
and New Hampshire, and then on to a new school
in the country, where I would not have to go back to
the city any more on Sunday nights.

With Pushkin in the forest.

It is early morning on a beautiful summer day.
Pushkin and I have been out since sunrise, taking
our usual path up the mountain: hopping the stones
across the stream, passing through the deep grass
of the field mowed by the neighboring farmer and

heading up into the young forest, making our way first through the maples, then the oaks, and, in the steepest section, a dazzling patch of white birches. I find the old stone wall that leads me to the summit of the mountain, and walk into the little clearing filled with brambles and sweet fern, at the center of which are two young white pines, tall enough to have dropped a thick carpet of fragrant brown needles at their bases, and wide-spreading enough to allow me room to sit beneath their branches. I sit cross-legged, looking down into the forest through which I've just walked, dazzled by the rising sun directly in front of me. The wind blows softly through the glistening pine needles. Chickadees call merrily nearby, and there's a sudden flutter and an arching flash of gold as a flicker speeds through the clearing. Beneath the stillness are the pulses and drones of a multitude of crickets and bees. I drink deeply from the peace and beauty of it all, and feel a rising sense of exaltation running warm and golden in my veins.

Seized by a sudden inspiration, deciding to ignore the warning voice in my mind that knows I am trespassing, and that someone—anyone—could come along at any moment, I pull my shirt over my head and slip out of my jeans and underpants, throwing them to the side so I can sit naked on the soft, warm pine needle carpet. The breeze that is blowing through the pines now plays gently on my pale skin, dappled by the sunshine radiating down through the glistening pine needles. I am sun and breeze, tree and bird. I am.

AIR

ON PRIVILEGE

When I think back over my childhood, I am struck by the depth of my pre-teen connection to the natural world. My awe and reverence for the beauty of the living beings and elements I saw around me was instinctive and deeply felt, strengthened by the sense of entrapment and revulsion I felt every time I had to leave my beloved countryside and return to the city. Although I hated that back-and-forth, unsettled lifestyle at the time, I now see that being forced to constantly feel the contrast of the city (which I hated) and the country (which I loved) gave me a unique vantage point—what Adrienne Rich called "outsider's eyes," or what Gloria Anzaldúa would call queer vision, the kind you can only get from a location in the borderlands, betwixt and between rather than fully immersed in any one place. Both Rich and Anzaldúa acknowledge that this position can be uncomfortable, but they also insist that it can be a place of visionary power. If I had grown up as the country girl I wished to be, I would not have known that anything else existed, and I might have taken the beautiful countryside for granted. Instead, I loved the natural world more and more every time I had to get in the car to leave it behind.

"Privilege is invisible to those who have it," Michael Kimmel and others have noted, and indeed, I only noticed my privilege when I was threatened with losing it. When a car accident nearly took my mother away from me, I suddenly realized how precious she was, and reacted by developing a neurotic fear of losing her. Other privileges I enjoyed without being aware of them as anything out of the ordinary. I took for granted my fairly gentle introduction to gender and sexuality and my parents' tolerance for my eccentricities. I saw as completely normal the way my family's white skin, intelligence and determined work ethic enabled my father's successful career, and the way his financial success cushioned us, allowing us the luxuries of both a country home and a safe, comfortable city apartment, plus a powerful car to bring us back and forth between them.

It wasn't until I was well into adulthood that I began to realize how my entire privileged childhood was made possible by my family's location in the comfortable heart of the American Empire. Growing up in an elite enclave of America is like growing up in a beautiful, well-managed gated community, with guards along the perimeter, and all one's needs taken care of—as long as your parents can pay. The thing about being raised inside such a space of privilege is that you don't even realize there are walls, with other people on the outside. Yes, as I got older I became aware that the people living on the other side of 96th Street were much less comfortable than we were, but they seemed very remote, almost as far away as the starving Ethiopians I read about in *The New York Times*. It was hard to even begin to understand their lives. As a child, I had no idea whatsoever that my comfortable lifestyle was built on the backs of other people's suffering, just as I had no idea, despite my reading of *Ranger Rick* and *National Wildlife*, that the delicious food my mother prepared every night for our dinner had been produced through the suffering of farm animals, the poisoning of insects, and ultimately the sickening of great swaths of the planet. As a child I was innocent and trusting, believing without question that adults and authorities were ethical and would do their best to safeguard me, my family, and the animals and natural world I loved.

Part of my training as a child growing up in Manhattan was learning to obey boundaries—not to go outside the bounds of the gated comfort zone my parents had created for our family, and not to ask uncomfortable questions about situations over which we were perceived to have no control. I also learned the peculiar peripheral vision of many city dwellers, by which we can walk the streets without making eye contact or really "seeing" those around us. There was so much I didn't see as a child, and so much I chose not to see as a young adult. As children, it's normal for us to simply try to grow and flower the best we can in the environment in which we've been planted. But part of growing up is overcoming that early ignorance and opening our eyes to the true contours of our social and physical landscapes.

The same mechanisms of invisible, unacknowledged privilege that structured my childhood are still guiding the attitudes of privileged American society writ large. Just as I went along for the ride without asking too many questions as a child, so many of us privileged citizens of America and the world have gone along for the globalized capitalist ride content to enjoy what we're given and careful not to ask too much about the foundations undergirding our wealth and comfort. What forests have been razed to provide the wood for the lovely lounge chairs out on the deck—or the deck itself, for that matter? How many children have worked their small fingers raw to knot the elegant Persian rug in the living room? How many indigenous people have been displaced to make way for the filthy aluminum mine that provides the shiny rolls of foil we so casually rip off, use and throw away in the course of preparing dinner? How many millions of songbirds have been lured to their deaths by the red blinking lights of the communications towers that pierce the skies at regular intervals all over the planet, placed there so we can text and chat and use our GPS systems wherever we are?

Questions like this are uncomfortable, and most of us would rather not ask them because we'd rather not think about the answers. So we focus on other things instead, like the next greatest gadget coming on to the market (*Did you get the new iPhone yet? Have you checked out those new plasma TVs?*) or the next vacation destination (*We went to St. Martin's last time. The beaches are fabulous!*) or what restaurant to go to for dinner (*I'm tired of Italian, let's try that new French place in Chelsea tonight*). Living the privileged life is just so enjoyable and easy, it's like growing up in the field of poppies in *The Wizard of Oz*, never even knowing there might be an alternative. Who needs to follow the yellow brick road when you're already home, enveloped in a sweet-smelling dream from which you never need or want to wake up?

Not until my life was more than half over did I suddenly wake up, stretch, and look around me, finally coming to see how privileged many of us Americans have been, during the past 50 years, to live under the pleasant delusion of limitless plenty. As a child, it never occurred to me to wonder where my next meal was coming from. I knew my mom would go to the store and buy everything she needed to prepare a wonderful home-cooked meal, day after day, year after year. Although the ease and abundance I was so fortunate to enjoy in my childhood may be unusual, most Americans share my indoctrination into believing in a backdrop of limitless resources. We assume that the superstores will never go empty, the gas pumps will never go dry, sunny days and rainy days will come in measured succession, and the trees will continue to produce the rich oxygen we all take for granted with every easy breath and heartbeat.

We humans still have a very childish relationship to the natural world. Just as in Shel Silverstein's disturbing children's book *The Giving Tree*, we believe, even in adulthood, that we are entitled to take and take from the natural world, rarely giving anything back. Like needy, self-absorbed children, we assume that Mother Earth will always be there to provide for us, and will always love us, no matter what we do.

WATER

ENTERING THE STREAM

With my brother away at camp and my parents away in the city for a few days, I'm left in the country by myself, just me and Pushkin. It's warm and summery out, and before she left Mom and I picked a big bucket of blueberries at a local farm, which I'm going to make into jam. I'm also working on digging out a couple of new perennial gardens, one in the corner by the house, where up to now only boring myrtle has been planted, and one up above the rock garden, where I've discovered a deep pocket of rich black earth in the rock ledge. For two days, I won't talk to anyone but Pushkin. I'll follow my own rhythms of eating, working and sleeping. I'll watch the wind fluttering in the maple leaves, and feel it moving through them to me, caressing my face gently. I will be at peace.

There was an abrupt dividing line between that last peaceful summer of my childhood, and the hurly-burly of young adulthood that began when I went away to college. From being a solitary, self-sufficient homebody, I stepped out of my quiet, cloistered existence into a completely different kind of environment. Although it was the late 1970s, the heady experimental air of the 1960s was still blowing strong on campus, along with patchouli incense, the scent of clove cigarettes, and sweet drifts of marijuana smoke. The fall of my first year in college, what pleased me most was the marvelous freedom of *not* getting on the highway to go "home" to the city on Sunday afternoons. For the first time in my life, I could watch the goldenrod and asters come into bloom at the end of the summer with equanimity; they were no longer the signal of my impending exile from the freedom and spaciousness of the country.

In the early weeks of my freshman year, I followed my old pattern of getting up at dawn to ramble through the dense forest on the hillside behind the dorm. It was quiet and ancient in there, strewn with mossy glacial boulders and overgrown with dark-green, sweetly scented hemlocks. I kept company with big flocks of chickadees and titmice that called to each other cheerfully as they flew from one patch of hemlock cones to another. But it wasn't long before the lure of human companionship grew strong, pulling me out of the forest and into smoke-filled dorm rooms crowded with young men and women, throbbing with the driving beats of The Who, Steely Dan and the Talking Heads.

At first we all took to each other with intense delight. We couldn't get enough of each other: we talked all night, went to class in the morning, then headed out to the woods in the afternoon to get high and talk some more. We hooked up, though that term had not yet been invented. We were mad with desire for that certain someone, and there was nothing to stop us from following our desires wherever they led. Parietals were very loose. Supervision was very permissive. As long as no one gets hurt....

I, who had been so solitary, such a dreamer, filled with romantic yearnings born of ballads and love stories rather than actual contact with real people, was easily swept into this much faster current. In the first few months at school I experienced my first kiss, oral sex, and intercourse—none of these with the same person. My mom helped me to get on the Pill, but could offer little guidance in how to navigate through the dizzying tangle of human relationships. I was so open, so eager to "fall in love" and be attached, to "have a boyfriend." Scare quotes because I really had no idea what these phrases meant, beyond what I had learned through reading novels.

I don't think young people who have come of age in the 21st century can appreciate how sheltered and innocent it was possible to be in the pre-Internet age. Even TV was simpler: there was no cable, no reality TV; there were only the three networks and PBS, and the programming was very limited. Movies were for special occasions, to be seen in the theater—there

Sixteen years old, Martha's Vineyard

were no VHS tapes, much less DVDs. There had been no substance abuse education or sex ed in my high school. So when I accepted my first joint from one of my new college friends, it was without any particular sense of transgression. I knew nothing about marijuana; not why it was illegal or where it came from, not even what could happen to me if I was caught with it. When I had sex for the first time, I knew nothing about STDs and was not worried about getting pregnant. I had never seen any pornography and knew nothing about technique. I simply followed my instincts, in my quiet naïve way, and if something felt good, I pursued it.

The problem with this untutored approach was that often I ended up following what seemed to be a clear, sunlit path, only to find myself suddenly lost in a dark, tangled stretch of undergrowth, dominated by confusion, depression and incomprehension. And no guides would appear to help me get through it. I just had to figure it out on my own.

My friend Gus has an idea I know is crazy, but I love it anyway: we're going to bring a garbage bag outside, gather all the dead pine needles we can find on the ground under the big pine trees outside his window, and bring them back into his tiny dorm room to make a fragrant nest on his floor. Laughing and gay, we do just that, piling the crisp dry pine needles a foot thick on top of the dull yellow carpet. Our labor done, Gus turns out the electric lights and carefully lights a candle on a shelf. We sit down in a room magically turned into a forest, and I have a sudden apprehension of my own power to transform what is into what could be. Lying back in the fragrant piney darkness, passing the bong, I am—happy.

But much of the time in those college years, I was not happy. Or rather, my happiness was very compartmentalized. I was happy when I was in class, especially my literature, writing and Spanish classes. Being happy outside of class, with my friends, was harder. The relationships were complicated and shifted so quickly, often seeming to demand of me more than I could deliver. I started to avoid going to the dining hall so I didn't have to make a decision about which people to sit with, or whether to take the risk of doing what I really wanted to do, which was to sit down at an empty table by myself.

In the winter of my first year at college, the friendships I had made so effortlessly back in the fall begin to crack with the strain of unmet expectations. Two young men are competing for my attention, my allegiance. I care about them both and do not want to have to choose between them. A third guy, meanwhile, is beginning to seem more and more appealing to me. Late at night, after a long confusing conversation, I head outside, heartsick, frustrated, hardly looking where I am going, fighting back tears. One of the guys trails behind me, still talking, trying to persuade me to shift my allegiance exclusively to him. Anger finally breaks through my confusion, and I speak to him sharply, asking to be left alone.

At that very moment, I feel a stabbing pain in my eye, and realize that I have just walked right into a sharp twig, protruding from a nearby tree and invisible in the darkness. I reel back, face in hands, and begin sobbing hysterically, all my self-control gone. When I open my eyes again, to make sure I can still see, the streetlight over by the pond is blurry. The contact lens in the poked eye is gone, and in these early days of contact lenses, it will be a while before I can get another one. I am sure this is the nadir of my existence, the worst day of my life. And there is nowhere to go but back to the dorm. No escape.

And yet I wanted so intensely to belong to a group, a tribe of people outside of my family, who would accept and approve of me. The group that I fell into and felt comfortable with at school were artists and musicians, kids who were not afraid to let their creativity flow out of them even if what they did with it was "weird." I was delighted by my friends' easy, unpretentious artistry: Ed's strange, magical drawings and dreamy piano improvisations, Frank's quirky short stories, or the way my friend Gus would take his cello outside and play classical improv music in the grass on a warm September afternoon.

But the young man who became my boyfriend
for most of my college years was not an artist. I was
attracted to him because he seemed more mature
than the others. He had his own car, was paying his
own way through school, and was essentially living
on his own, with little help from his family back in
the Midwest. He was also more influenced by the
remnants of 1960s counterculture than anyone
else I knew. The youngest of five children, he had
learned about sex, drugs and rock'n'roll from his
older brother and sisters, who had actually lived
the counterculture as teenagers. His hippie glamour
appealed to me—his long hair, silver pinkie ring,
John Lennon glasses and stick-shift VW bus, on
which I learned to drive in a big parking lot one
winter. We became a pair in the second semester of
my freshman year, and stayed together, rockily, for
the next four years.

*Through one of my dad's connections, I get an intern-
ship as a reporter at a local weekly newspaper. On
my very first day, the sweet and energetic editor
sends me out to do an interview at a landmark
church that is being renovated. I drive over to the
church in the 1973 yellow VW Squareback that
my dad bought me when I got my license, and take
some pictures with the Nikkormat SLR camera my
mom handed down to me; I've been taking photo-
graphy at school, and not only know how to load
the Tri-X film, but also how to develop it and make*

prints on the old enlargers crowded together in the red-lit darkroom.

I talk with the couple who are in charge of the renovations at the church, drive back to the office on Main Street, sit down at one of the grimy, chunky DOS computers, with the green letters glowing dimly against the black monitor background, and type up my story in one sitting. Reading it over when I'm done, the editor is impressed, and I am thrilled when it runs on the front page that Thursday, together with one of the pictures I took, blown up large. Just like that, I'm a reporter.

I loved my newspaper internship. I became a regular correspondent, covering town meetings and finding out from the inside what small town politics were all about. I reviewed concerts and plays and spent many hours going through press releases to create the weekly summer arts calendar. My newspaper colleagues were quirky, interesting, and all much older than me—they treated me kindly, teaching me the tricks of the trade with patience and enthusiasm.

When I started college, I had the intention of majoring in environmental studies, knowing that I cared about nothing so much as the natural world. But when I took Introduction to Environmental Studies, I found learning about environmental rules and regulations dry; and although I loved the field trips we took for the Principles of Ecology class, exploring beautiful New England mountaintops and fields, I had no use for counting all the species in 12-inch or 12-foot squares. When my Animal Behavior professor assigned us to pick a local animal to observe and write about, I immediately chose my friends the chickadees—I knew just where to find them in the woods and I loved to follow them around on cool, foggy early mornings. But my rapturous mornings in the forest earned me only a B on the final paper—the first B I'd ever gotten in my straight-A life. Math and statistics were total road blocks: I struggled to attain a C in math my first semester, and then successfully begged my way out of the rest of the year-long requirement in math, beating a hasty retreat into the English classes where I knew I could excel. No one ever suggested to me that perhaps nature or environmental writing might be a way I could channel my love of the natural world into a career path. I stopped going out in the morning to follow the chickadees, spending more and more of my time poring over books in my small, dusty dorm room.

In my sophomore year, I fell under the spell of Virginia Woolf, who seemed, more than any other writer I'd encountered, to be able to bring into language the full complexity of human perception and experience. When I read her description in *To the Lighthouse* of how Mrs. Ramsay would sink down into a "wedge-shaped core of darkness" when she had a quiet moment alone after the hustle-bustle of her busy household, I knew exactly what Woolf was talking about. I too still craved those moments when I could let my public persona drop and simply *be*, growing still and quiet, open to the stroking fingers of the breeze, or in Mrs. Ramsay's case, the ray of the lighthouse. But those moments came to me ever more rarely.

In my junior year of college, with my parents' support, I move off-campus so I can have Pushkin with me. I share a log-cabin style house with my boyfriend Alan and two other guys. It's my first chance to make a home on my own, and I enjoy setting up the kitchen, buying groceries, getting into a domestic routine with my housemates, who seem to enjoy it too. One cold winter night, we throw a party and our living room fills up with a crowd of students, most of whom I hardly know. Joints and bongs pass hand to hand; laughter rumbles from the guys and trills from the girls.

At some point, very late, Alan and I notice that there is a brilliant full moon outside, and we get a sudden impulse to go cross-country skiing in the big snowy fields just up the road from our house. The frosty air feels like another element entirely, like diving into cold water after the overheated, smoky atmosphere of our people-filled house. It is silent outside. The moon is riding high and remote in the sky, reflecting so brightly off the snow-covered fields that we have no trouble at all making our way. We strap on our skis and climb the hillside with quiet determination,

Pushkin romping and playing joyfully in the snow alongside us.

At the top, we turn and suddenly shift modes, from awkward uphill sideways marching to flying lightly and swiftly down the rolling snow meadow. Alan lets out whoops of glee and Pushkin starts barking as he struggles through the drifts, trying to keep up. I hang back a moment, pausing to survey the moon-washed landscape and glittering stars hanging low in the distance. I inhale deeply and exhale with a whoosh, trying to cleanse the smokiness from my lungs and take the cold glory of this moment deep inside me. I feel a rare sense of exultation and freedom. I don't want to go back inside.

In my senior year, Alan and I rented another house together, just the two of us and Pushkin. Although it felt like a big step towards adulthood, we weren't very happy together in that house. I was happiest sitting alone with Pushkin at my feet, working on my senior thesis on androgyny in the novels of Virginia Woolf. I had become fascinated by a passage in *A Room of One's Own* where Woolf describes the ideal writer as androgynous—not male or female, but partaking of the best qualities of both. She gave Shakespeare as her example of a fine androgynous writer, and my thesis explored the question of whether she herself lived up to her ideal and wrote androgynous novels. Queer theory had not yet been invented; the closest I could get for guidance was literary criticism by Carolyn Heilbrun and Dorothy Dinnerstein, who talked about masculine and feminine patterns in literature. I read all of Woolf's work closely, taking extensive notes by hand, and found that she tended to balance the masculine and feminine in her characters, and to challenge the convention that masculinity equals active and aggressive, while femininity equals passive and submissive. It was a fascinating topic, absorbing and engaging me completely all that long cold winter. I finished typing my thesis and turned it in to my advisors with a tremendous sense of accomplishment and satisfaction.

In the spring of my senior year in college, Alan and I are driving to my parents' house in Manhattan, and we are having an interminable discussion/ argument. I am driving. He is in the passenger seat next to me. On and on it goes, all the way down the highway, on to the Saw Mill Parkway, and finally we're driving through the city streets, up Park Avenue to 93rd Street. I wish he wasn't with me. I don't want to have to face my parents in such an emotional state. I feel strung tight like a bow, and completely exhausted.

Our argument reaches a climax of intensity, and I won't bend to whatever it is Alan wants me to agree to. All of a sudden he turns to me with a snarl of rage, and smacks me hard on the knee, on the leg controlling the accelerator. It hurts! I look at him, stunned, and immediately pull over to the side of Park Avenue. I am shaking with shock and rage. He hit me? He hit me! He is looking shocked too, and backpedaling fast. I just want him out of the car, I never want to see him again. But do I make that happen? No. I allow him to apologize, I allow him to make it up to me, I allow him to continue at my side. We pull ourselves together and put on a good front for my parents. We go on.

And so began a long line of experiences in which I remained in situations or attachments that were unhealthy for me because—why? Because it was easier to stay than to go. I resisted change and was loyal to a fault. Throughout my childhood and adolescence, my parents used to tease me by calling me a "mollusk" because I was so tightly attached to the rock of the family, and I was a shy loner, peering out tentatively at the world. Even after I left home for college, those traits persisted. When I made friends, I expected them to be my friends forever, and was hurt—so, so hurt—when they were able to casually leave me behind. I held on to my relationship with my boyfriend even when he did everything possible to indicate that he wanted to be free of me.

After graduation, I started working fulltime as a reporter at a daily newspaper in Connecticut. Things were fine at work, but not fine at home. I was unhappy in my relationship, but could not bring myself to walk away. I crouched in my corner and waited for him to make that move. The day he came in and told me, in way too much detail, about how much fun he'd had on his latest sexual adventure—which had taken place in the little house we were renting together—was the day it was finally clear to me that our connection had to end. I drowned my sadness and disappointment in great gulps of marijuana smoke, but I knew it was time. I had to move on.

It's a cool August night, almost a year after I graduated from college and began working fulltime as a reporter. Thinking I might like to be a foreign correspondent, I've decided to go into a Master's program in International Relations at American University. Alone in the country, and getting ready to leave for Washington D.C in a few days, I'm feeling a bit nervous and restless. On a whim, I do something uncharacteristic: I pick up the phone and call one of my reporter friends at his office, knowing he works the evening shift. Shyly, I suggest that we meet on a local hill to watch the shooting stars. When he agrees, I throw a tarp and sleeping bags into the back of my car, grab a freshly rolled joint, and drive out into the deep, velvety darkness, where the stars are glowing like brilliant lamps overhead. When he arrives, we carry the blankets out to the middle of the grassy field, setting the tarp down carefully so that the thick dew of the August night doesn't soak through the sleeping bags.

We lie down together under those incandescent stars and begin passing the joint back and forth. Every few seconds a brilliant star shoots across the sky overhead with an almost-audible whoosh. Before long I feel a hand stroking my breasts tentatively and then he turns, catching me in a devouring kiss. He is in his thirties and married to a woman he loves. I am not yet 23, my college boyfriend is gone and I'm yearning for romance. But this doesn't feel right. I can't stop thinking about his wife. I know that going any further than a kiss and a fondle would be a mistake. I turn away from him firmly, feeling his disappointment and frustration but not relenting. We lie there a while longer, finishing the joint, watching the stars, holding hands loosely under the blankets. When we pack up in the darkness and make our way silently back to the cars, meteors continuing to sizzle overhead, I know I won't see him again.

After one week of trying to find an apartment in the unbearable August heat of Washington D.C. and attending the first few classes at American University, I realized I was in the wrong place. Withdrawing from the graduate program, I fled back home to my parents, and found myself, for the first time in five years, living in my old bedroom at 1185 Park Avenue. It was quiet and comfortable there; it felt like a safe harbor in which to collect myself and figure out what to do next. I kept myself amused by tapping out some short stories on my self-correcting typewriter, Pushkin at my feet, and pored over the Sunday *New York Times* Help Wanted section, looking for a job as a reporter or writer.

I landed the first job I applied for, as a staff writer for a monthly national magazine for sheriffs and police chiefs. It was a small staff—just me, the editor and the publisher, plus a student intern or two. The job was interesting, involving reading through the national press for police-related news, making lots of long-distance telephone calls to police chiefs to gather quotes and more information, then writing it all up for publication. On our staff of three I was by far the youngest, but we quickly struck up a camaraderie based on long lunch-hour walks to the piers to share a joint before returning to work for the afternoon. The irony of this was not lost on me: here we were, three potheads, covering law enforcement news.

I have just had dinner in midtown with my friend Nancy, and saying goodbye I quickly flag down a cab and hop in, settling my red cashmere coat around me, my Coach bag on my lap. The cabdriver heads down Central Park South and turns up into the park, leaving the glitter of midtown lights and glass behind. The surging power of the car, moving smoothly and swiftly uptown, matches my sense of personal power as an attractive, independent young woman with money in my wallet and places to go, people to see. Nancy and I are planning a spring trip to Greece together, and I am excited to think of traveling to Europe for the first time. The world seems full of promise and possibility, as though a red carpet is rolling out comfortably in front of me everywhere I go.

In the 1980s, among yuppies like me, New York City was humming with vitality and promise. It was as if I had slipped into a swiftly moving current that could carry me just about anywhere I wanted to go. I loved living at home with my parents again; getting up to the familiar sound of my dad scuffing briskly down the hallway in his bathrobe and slippers, flicking on the WQXR news as he rounded the corner into the sunny kitchen to grab his coffee and bagel. I loved taking Pushkin down the elevator and out through the courtyard for his morning walk, the sparrows twittering as they built their nests in the streetlights, the yellow taxis cruising hopefully up and down Park Avenue, men emerging from the buildings with their briefcases in hand, striding with determination and power out to their chauffeured cars, or, in my father's case, down to the subway.

I too would head out early for work, wearing my sneakers and socks over my stockings, carrying my heels in my bag—most days I walked to work, enjoying the long straight promenade down leafy Fifth Avenue, by Central Park. After a year or so I moved on, thanks to my father's connections, to a plum little job at an upscale business magazine. I was the "managing editor," but the staff was all freelance and the publisher, my boss, was rarely around, so I was essentially on my own in a magnificent Fifth Avenue corner office, with huge windows looking south towards the World Trade Center and west towards the Hudson River. The work wasn't hard, the pay was good, and I had time to start dabbling in some night classes, first in creative writing at the New School, and then in English literature at New York University. I hadn't lost my ambition to be a Writer with a capital W, more than just a journalist whose work would be used as waste paper the day after it was published. But I was painfully aware of having no mentors, no peer community, not even any contemporary writers whose work I wanted to emulate. It seemed to me that I needed to get back in school.

Tentatively, I sidle into the brightly lit, high-ceilinged New York University classroom overlooking Washington Square, from which the melancholy notes of a lone saxophone rise like a soundtrack. I've signed up to take a class in Modern British Literature, having already tried and rejected as too intimidating the creative writing classes over at the New School, and having been turned down by the Journalism school at Columbia University. The professor walks up to the desk at the front of the room, casual in jeans and a loosely buttoned shirt, his wispy blond shoulder-length hair contrasting oddly with the big bald dome of his head. He sits down at the desk, pulls out a pack of Marlboros, a book of matches and a small note card, on which he has jotted a few words. He lights up and begins to talk earnestly, sardonically, hypnotically, about the topic of the day: Matthew Arnold's ongoing argument with Walter Pater, as seen through the lens of Jacques Derrida. I understand nothing of what he says, but I love the passion and intensity of his teaching style and I pick up the challenge he throws down like an invitation to a duel, determined to learn his language so I can meet him on his intellectual turf. I settle into an arid, completely artificial landscape populated by glamorous and ferociously intelligent people. My new home.

I plunged into the intellectual world of literary studies at NYU wholeheartedly, relishing the challenge of learning the complex language of post-structuralist theory, in French, Spanish and German as well as English. It never occurred to me to question why my own innate voice was considered uninteresting, unsophisticated and unimportant here, or why all the heavy hitters in this strange new world of poststructuralist literary theory were men, with a few token honorary exceptions—women like me who were willing to walk the walk and talk the talk to be accepted.

I am sitting outside my advisor's office, waiting for a meeting to discuss my master's thesis, a comparative study of Flaubert's Salammbô *and Poe's "The Fall of the House of Usher." I am dressed to please in a tight skirt, tall black boots and a button-down shirt casually arranged to intimate my cleavage. My advisor—the same bald, cigarette-smoking prof I had been following since my very first class—pokes his head out of the door just as an older man strolls up, giving me a quick appraising glance from beneath his bushy white eyebrows as he passes. As the two men shake hands and retreat into the office, I hear a snatch of conversation: "Who's that?" "An advisee..." "Hm, nice advisee!" The tone is lascivious. Later I am intro-duced briefly, and realize with a start known only to shy graduate students that this rumpled-looking old gentleman is none other than the one of the most famous literary critics in New York at the time. His offhand comment, not meant for my ears, makes me smile—I'm glad he noticed me. Nice advisee....*

What I was supposed to do, as a reasonably attrac-tive, well-educated, well-groomed young woman, was to find a suitable partner: someone who had been raised more or less as I had been, with care and cul-tivation, who had gotten a good education and was now finding his stride in law or medicine or busi-ness. I was supposed to follow the model my parents had set, in other words. Although I took my work as a budding academic seriously, I always assumed that I would marry, have children and make parenting my priority, while my partner focused on bringing home the bacon—the same arrangement that seemed to have worked so well for my parents. I never spelled this out to myself concretely, but in an unspoken way, I expected to be able to have a career on my own terms, meaning that I would be able to work part-time while my children were small, or even not work for money at all, devoting myself to my writing craft the way my mother had devoted herself to her ceramics, without worrying about whether or not she was making money at it.

There was just one small problem with these expectations: I was not interested in the kind of men who would have been able to provide me with such a scenario. Or at least, not the ones I was able to meet. I was still attracted to artsy types, to quirky individualists who focused on exploring their passions rather than on building a career. When I think back on the string of young men I went out with in my early twenties, I see myself rejecting, over and over, the guys who could have given me the lifestyle to which I was accustomed as my parents' daughter. I was looking for something else: a certain spark, someone who could take me out of my old, well-worn grooves and patterns. Someone who could make me feel really special, and especially alive. Not a white knight, exactly—I didn't need rescuing—but some who could take me on an exciting ride. Such a person was a) hard to find and b) incompatible with my simultaneous expectations of a conventional, stable future family life. Sometimes, wandering by myself in my parents' big, elegant apartment, I felt as though I was walled off from the rest of humanity, ever destined to be alone. What if I never found my life partner, Mr. Right? I could not imagine being content to forge a life for myself alone.

With the support of my parents, I've arranged to rent a friend's apartment in Paris for the summer while I take French classes at the Alliance Francaise—I have shifted from English to Comparative Literature at NYU, and need to get my French up to speed quickly. After a few days in London, I take the train over to Paris. This is the first time I've traveled to Europe by myself and I'm nervous but excited, enjoying the challenge of finding my way through unfamiliar territory.

Once settled in my big, bright apartment in a gracious old building in the 14th arrondissement, I slip into a pleasant routine, walking down Boulevard du Sebastopol every morning, over the bridges by the churches of Sainte Chapelle and Notre Dame, grabbing a coffee and baguette avec jambon to eat in the peaceful Jardin du Luxembourg before making my way along Boulevard Raspail to the Alliance. The classes, which run from 10 a.m. to 3 p.m. with an hour off for lunch, are run by serious, hardworking teachers who insist on complete attention at all times. I love the intensity of it, and can feel my French improving daily. One morning, when I wake up and realize that I've just been dreaming in French, I'm elated—I like myself in French much more than I have liked myself

in English or Spanish. It's such a glamorous, sophisti-
cated language.

I ended up extending my stay in Paris, aided
by my obliging parents, Francophiles themselves,
who came over to visit during the summer and saw
how happy I was in my new environment. Paris was
so beautiful, like a living dream—to be there while
the chestnut leaves turned yellow in the Jardin du
Luxembourg, to wander about the cobbled streets
of the Ile St. Louie on a foggy October morning,
to cross over the Pont Neuf as the lights were just
coming on at dusk...it was like living in one of the
grainy French films that had mesmerized me back in
New York. I inhaled the spirit of Paris deeply, filled
with nostalgia even while I was still there, knowing
that I was living through some of the most intensely
marvelous days of my life.

But I didn't find love there. I found Iranian
men eager to get to know any American girl in the
hope of obtaining a green card, and I found some
crazy young Australian dentists, living the high life
in Paris before returning to start their staid dental
practices back home. They were fun to hang out
with, but that's as far as it went. As the days short-
ened and the darkness grew, it was looking like I'd
probably be going back to New York without having
had the grand Parisian romance I'd come to expect
from watching all those great films. And then the
Mexican earthquake struck.

Walking down the Boulevard Raspail on my way to my morning class at the Alliance Francaise, I pause at a kiosk, drawn by the huge headlines on the front page of Le Monde: Tremblement du Terre Massif en Mexique. *Remembering that one of my classmates is Mexican, I buy the paper, and before class starts I walk over to show it to him, asking if he's heard the news. Startled, alarmed, and appreciative, he runs to try to call his parents in Mexico City, where all the damage is said to have occurred, but he can't get through. We learn that the phone lines are all down. It is 1985 and there is no World Wide Web to rely on— he is isolated and worried, and I am suddenly caught up in his story. After class, we go for a glass of vin blanc et tarte tatin at a nearby patisserie, and I find him charming, compelling, his dark eyes intense and passionate beneath a thick fringe of black eyelashes, his Latino/indigenous features craggy and beautiful to me. There is a strange moment, when we descend into the Metro on opposite sides of the track to go our separate ways home; we lock eyes across the unbreachable gulf of the tracks and I feel a depth of connection entirely out of proportion to our brief acquaintance. He suddenly seems like someone I know, or am meant to know, and the parting is unexpectedly wrenching. I go home feeling melancholy in the knowledge that he will be leaving on the next available plane for Mexico, and it's unlikely I will ever see him again.*

Several weeks later, the phone rings in my apartment one evening and when I answer it I am greeted by Teo's deep, warm voice, entreating me to come to Mexico to visit him. I'll think about it, I tell him. But my heart says yes.

And so instead of going to Spain with my friend Diana, I ended up going home to New York for Christmas, and then making plans to go visit Teo in Mexico City. Here is a moment in my life history that I always wonder about: how was it that my parents were so blasé about my traveling alone to Mexico to visit my new friend Teo, whom they had never met? They didn't even bother to get the phone number of his parents' house, where I would be staying, or my flight information. Off I flew to Mexico City, and a week later I returned, head over heels—*bouleversée*, as the French would say—in love.

Teo's family was part of the aspiring Mexican middle class. His mother's father had been a successful businessman who owned a thread factory in the first half of the 20th century. Her family lived in a big colonial house in the south of Mexico City, where, for the seven girls in the family of thirteen kids, life was about learning to cook, doing the laundry, and waiting to find the right husband. Teo's father grew up on a little subsistence farm in a small village on the outskirts of the city, the son of an alcoholic father who died young and a strong *campesina* mother who raised turkeys, cultivated corn and always wore her hair in a long braid down the middle of her back. Of her children, only Prudencio, Teo's father, was ambitious enough to head down into Mexico City to go to the public university and make a bid for a different kind of life. He became an accountant and worked for a rising politician from a wealthy family—they greased each other's wheels and rose together, Prudencio marrying Carla, the facto-ry-owner's daughter, and raising his family of four sons and a daughter in a house with four bedrooms, three bathrooms, a modern kitchen and marble floors—quite an achievement for a boy who grew up in a dirt-floor *rancho* in the mountains.

Visiting Mexico was an eye-opening experience for me. I was used to seeing homeless people in Manhattan, sleeping in cartons on the park benches along Fifth Avenue, or wandering around wild-eyed, clearly psychotic and in need of help. But the poverty in Mexico was different. It couldn't be blamed on personal failing because it was so prevalent. Everywhere you looked you saw starving dogs and cats rooting for scraps and gangs of frantic children lining up at the traffic inter-sections to wash windshields or, even worse, to stick lit kerosene-soaked rags down their throats, all in the hopes of earning a penny or two from the wealthy folks passing by in their fancy cars. I was horrified and fascinated by the callous way the rich people were able to totally ignore suffering, whether of children or sweet little kittens, obvi-ously starving to death.

I am visiting Teo for Semana Santa, and on Easter weekend he takes me in his sleek Jetta on a road trip up to Valle de Bravo, a resort town on a lake in the pine-forested mountains above Mexico City. We check into a lovely colonial hotel, have a great meal with outstanding Spanish wine, and spend an amorous night. The next morning, we take a walk in the forest by the lake, bringing with us a little picnic: some cheese, bread and a large papaya that Teo had bought the day before from a roadside stand, and left in the trunk of the car overnight. We spread a blanket on a sunny spot on a hillside with a view of the lake, the deep fragrance of the pines providing a heady, intoxicating aroma. Teo strums his guitar and sings romantic Spanish boleros, gazing deeply into my eyes; I feel like I'm in a heavenly dream.

Suddenly, like forest sprites, a group of little brown children appear, with unkempt hair, ragged clothing and bright, pleading eyes. They kneel at the edge of the clearing and watch us cautiously for a while, then creep closer, chattering softly amongst themselves in an unfamiliar language—not Spanish, something more musical. Teo puts his guitar down and speaks to them kindly. "Shall we give them the rest of the papaya?" he asks me. It was all that remained of our picnic. I think about the sweet, dark orange flesh of the papaya and shake my head; I want to eat more of that myself! A shadow of disapproval passes across his face, but he simply picks up the big papaya—it's huge, bigger than a football—cuts off a small piece and gives it to the children, and shoulders the rest. We fold up our blanket and return to the car, the magic of the moment broken. On the way to the car, there is another discordant moment: I nearly step into a large pile of human excrement left behind a tree. I am angry—how can people defile these beautiful woods like that? At home it would never happen. Mexico is so beautiful, and yet so disappointing.

As we drive to Teo's father's family home, about two hours away, the hungry, intense eyes of the woodland children haunt me, and I begin to feel sick. By the time we arrive, I have fever, chills and my stomach is cramping in violent diarrhea. Instead of joining in the big family Easter party, I take to the nearest bed, and Teo runs around trying to find a doctor willing to attend me in the midst of the festivities. As I lie there in fetal position, curled up around my painful, gurgling intestines, feeling sorry for myself, I know what's going on. It's the papaya. We had cut into it and left it sitting open in the car overnight, where it had probably spoiled. But I know that's not the real reason I got sick. It was divine retribution, for not sharing the fruit with the children, for being so selfish that I ignored their obvious hunger to satisfy my own plump, well-fed desires.

I was far from being able to process and understand the flash of intuition I got that day, telling me that I needed to take a good hard look at my own social position in the world. In my twenties,

I was still coasting along, enjoying the ride. I had moved into a studio apartment at 24 Fifth Avenue, which my parents bought from a friend while I was in Paris. It had a great view looking west over the roofs and gardens of the brownstones along 9th and 10th streets, towards the tall red brick clock tower on Sixth Avenue, and it was just around the corner from my classes at NYU. I took a part-time job as an assistant editor for the monthly newsletter of the Institute for International Education, the organization that administers the Fulbright grants worldwide, and walked to work a few days a week, enjoying the cityscape as I made my way past Gramercy Park over to First Avenue, past the United Nations to my office building.

For my birthday I got my first computer, a bulky DOS machine that took me a long time to learn how to use, and a slow ink-jet printer. I set it up and began writing an intense, sexy autobiographical novel I called *Jubilant Uncertainty*, along with literary papers my professors told me were "brilliant," bestowing on me over and over warmly approving A's. Doors were opened for me. I was invited to the oh-so-elegant soirees at my professors' Soho lofts, where I could sip white wine, make witty conversation, and pose in my chic downtown outfits with the best of them. I wrote long letters to my best friend Rachele, who lived in Vancouver but sometimes joined us upstate in the summer, or on our annual pilgrimage to Martha's Vineyard. I waited eagerly for the next passionate love letter from Teo, who was still in Mexico, saving money to visit me in New York. Life was good.

It's the third week of August, and we've been at the Vineyard already for two weeks. This summer my parents have rented Clarissa's house in Chilmark for the entire month of August. Dad goes back into the city now and then from the little airport in Edgartown, and spends hours on the phone working in the mornings, but we always manage to get to our beach, Lucy Vincent, by around 10 a.m., before the parking lot fills up. Once parked, we load ourselves up with towels and beach blankets, a big cooler with sandwiches, fruit and drinks, and bags of books and suntan lotion, and head onto the sandy, sweet-smelling path to the beach. There's always a little haze out over the swelling waves of the cold, salty Atlantic, and the glistening pebbles roll up and down rhythmically in the tide as we kick off our shoes and begin the long walk along the hard-packed sand, all the way to the far end of the beach, where the cliffs end and the fine white sand is wide and flat, with grassy dunes and a lagoon in the back. We'll be there all day, enjoying the hot sun, the warm, soft sand, the cool, rolling waves, the gulls drifting by....until finally, in the late afternoon, with the sun setting and the tide coming in, we'll walk back down the beach, dazed by the sun, toned by the waves, and absolutely peaceful after another long day of reading, sleeping, and staring out over the ocean.

Every afternoon we go straight from the beach to the fish market in Lambert's Cove, where the ice-filled cases are heaped with huge swordfish steaks, piles of sweet flounder, tanks of lively lobsters and big buckets of clams and mussels. We pick out our dinner and go home to take turns in the warm outdoor shower, gathering in the kitchen to sip gin-and- tonics and help Mom with the cooking, listening to Bonnie Raitt or James Taylor on the battered cassette deck. We eat a delicious dinner, play guitar and sing for a while with Dad, go to bed and get up to do it all over again the next day. Perfect abundance, happiness, peace. The only sadness comes during the last few days at the beach, when my "moaming" begins in anticipation of having to say goodbye to it all until the next year.

Life seemed like it could just drift on pleasantly this way, indefinitely. It was a total shock, late one summer afternoon, to find myself lying down in the back of my parents' car on the way upstate, burning with fever and feeling utterly wretched, sicker than I'd ever been in my life. It was so abrupt: one day I was fine, going about my business at NYU and enjoying the pleasures of living on my own in Greenwich Village; the next day I was an invalid. Just like that.

I am lying on the couch in the den in my parents' apartment at 1185, under the blue and black crocheted blanket I've loved all my life. The distant roar of the city is remote and the empty apartment is quiet:

my parents are out, my brother off at college. From time to time one of the cats strolls by and looks at me strangely: what am I doing there, lying endlessly on the couch?

I have mono. It came on me so suddenly at the end of the summer—the high fever with chills, the absolute exhaustion. I am determined to keep going to my classes at NYU, but I can't live alone. I can just barely manage to function, moving as I do through a thick fog of physical and mental fatigue. So I move back into my bedroom at 1185, going down to NYU by cab twice a week for my classes, spending the rest of the time reading and sleeping in bed or on the couch. I eat endless bowls of my mom's special beef mushroom barley soup, which we call Grandma's soup because her mother used to make it, and my Russian great-grandma before her. It's made by boiling beef bones for hours, and I must be craving the iron in it because I eat it every day, ravenously—that soup and nothing else.

I recline under the afghan, reading Flaubert's Madame Bovary in French and waiting impatiently for the next letter from Teo to arrive, carefully written in black ink on blue airmail envelope/letter paper, bearing colorful Mexican stamps like exotic tattoos. He writes in French, the language we both love and in which we first conversed, and with each "Je t'aime" I read I fall more and more in love with him. I am determined to get better by spring so I can go to Mexico to visit him again during the summer. Meanwhile the *clock ticks slowly and the cats curl up on my lap as I read long French novels and write elaborate deconstructions of them for my final papers. I feel I am caught in some sluggish backwater of my life; I can see the fast-moving river glinting in the distance, but I can't reach it. I sleep. I sleep.*

The mono held me in its bear hug for nearly a year. But in the end it let me go, and I continued on my path, finishing my Masters in Comparative Literature and writing my thesis on the trope of the veil in Flaubert and Poe, elegantly argued in fluent post-structuralese. I was welcomed into the doctoral program in Comp Lit with full tuition remission and a graduate teaching assistantship, and started teaching in the Expository Writing Program. When Teo visited me in New York and waited for me in my little studio apartment while I went to class, I would go through my day hugging to myself the secret smiling delight that threatened to tingle out through every pore, the anticipation of the moment when I would once again be clasped in his arms. Even the great sorrow of Pushkin's death—he died at age 11, after a short illness—could not deflate my buoyant feeling that I had found my life partner at last—that my *real* life was about to begin.

Teo had been learning English and French and saving money to travel since he was a teenager, the only one in his whole big extended family to be interested in looking beyond the parochial borders of family and nation. Thanks to his father's connections, he found government jobs as a lawyer easily, and was able to drop them to travel frequently, secure in the knowledge that when he had used up all his money, he could always come back to his family home, find another job and start saving again. I knew, because he told me, that on these trips abroad he was constantly searching for Ms. Right—a blonde, blue-eyed girl who had the right combination of charms and talents: attractive, good at homemaking, smart enough to have a career. That was me, wasn't it? My family background also impressed him, making him think that the transition from Mexican lawyer to New York banker or businessman could be accomplished easily with the help of his affable new father-in-law.

I was not so calculating. I only knew that when I was with him, I felt happier and more alive than at any other time. In the summer of 1987, I went to stay with him at his parents' house for a few weeks and was warmly welcomed by his family. His mom, a wonderful cook who made a different entrée every day for weeks without ever needing to consult a cookbook, taught me how to make guacamole and red rice, and I watched with interest as she and her daughter spent days preparing special festive dishes like *mole con pollo* or *pozole*. As a guest, I was never allowed to do any dishes; I sat at the table with Teo and his father and brothers while his mother and sister went back and forth from the kitchen, serving and clearing.

During the weekdays, when Teo went off to work, I would drive his VW Jetta through the scary traffic over to UNAM, the National Autonomous University of Mexico, to take classes in Mexican literature and cultural history. On weekends, Teo taught me to dance salsa and cumbia on the smooth white marble floor of his parents' living room, surrounding by twirling, smiling couples of all ages, all of us feeling smooth and relaxed on endless rum and cokes. As *la gringa*, I was always an object of special attention, considered beautiful by virtue of my blonde hair and blue eyes, and a special catch for Teo, who treated me with gentlemanly courtesy in public, and hot desire in private. I felt special—attractive, unique and interesting—in a way I never had before. No one in this environment cared much about my brains or my career—it was enough that I was American, blonde, and cultivated. *La novia de Teo.*

Memories of Mexico

It is the summer of 1988 and I am living for a couple of months with Teo in an apartment he's rented for us in Mexico City. During the day, he goes off to his job as a lawyer for the Ministry of Education, and I stay home and read one of the many volumes of A la recherché du temps perdu in French, a delicious, languorous activity. On weekends we meet his friends to go dancing at big, glittering salsa clubs, or go driving outside the city to explore picturesque little Mexican towns.

One day we meet up with Teo's friend Alberto, who invites us to come with him to a house in the country he says he's rented. It turns out to be a beautiful colonial mansion in a small town, full of dark polished wood beams and antiques, built around a magnificent central garden. I am walking around inside, admiring the house, when there is a sudden explosion of Spanish and Teo is hustling me out a back door at a run. Later he tells me, somewhat embarrassed, that in fact Alberto hadn't rented the place, but had broken into it, and the police had shown up.

Another time, after a night on the town, Teo is driving us home and I'm nervous because he's high as a kite on rum and cokes—I'm just praying he can stay on the road and get us home safely. Suddenly he pulls off the highway and rolls to a stop in front of a lit-up building, a synagogue, suggesting we take a look around. I'd rather just go home, but he won't be dissuaded, and I've learned not to argue with him when he's drunk. I try to understand what he's saying, and placate him—it's something about the behavior of the Jews in Mexico—but he's way too far gone to hear what I'm saying, so gradually I just submit and let him spend his fury in what seems to be an endless rant.

Eventually we are back in the car. I can't take the wheel because I am totally lost driving in Mexico City, so I am at his mercy. He manages to pilot us *home safely before passing out, but I am stone cold sober, shaking with rage and not sleepy at all. We are back at his parents' house at this point, just a day or two before we're due to return to New York to make the final arrangements for our wedding. I sit in the dark on the couch downstairs, bitterly upset and worried about the path I've chosen. Am I making a huge mistake? Can I marry a man who gets so entirely out of control when drunk? What am I getting myself into? Am I out of my mind?*

In the morning he gets up and starts drinking beer, his go-to cure for wicked hangovers. He doesn't remember anything, he says, about what happened the night before, and when he sees how upset I am, he's totally contrite, begging my pardon in his most loving, winning way. There's a part of me that knows I will never be able to trust him. But I already feel too connected to him to pull away. I can't face the deep sense of loss I know would result if we broke up now. I don't want to be alone again in New York, waiting for Mr. Right. I'm going to marry him.

We were married at the United Nations Chapel in New York, by a woman Ethical Culture minister. I wore a slim, stylish white silk dress; Teo wore a black tux with a red rose in the lapel. We rode to the chapel in separate limos, me with my maid of honor, he with his parents and two younger siblings, who had come up to New York for the wedding. After the ceremony, which I wrote with the minister,

some hundred friends and family from my side piled into my parents' apartment for the elegant catered party, complete with garlands of flowers, dancing and champagne toasts. Everyone was so happy. It was such a happy day.

Afterwards, we slipped into the swift current of married life easily. Without thinking much about it, he and I fell into the same patterns we'd been raised in: he got dressed in a suit and tie every morning and headed off for work (he'd been hired, with the help of his dad's connections, at a Mexican bank) and I cleaned up the breakfast dishes, went about my graduate school days of classes, meetings and studying, and had a good balanced dinner on the table almost every night. I tried to convince Teo to go to law school, since his Mexican law degree was useless in the U.S., but he was not interested in returning to school. For success he relied on his greatest asset: charm.

Teo and I are having a party in our tiny studio apartment. We've invited eight of our closest friends, and I've spent two days shopping and preparing the meal, an authentic tinga poblana, *a tender pork stew in a thick, spicy red sauce. I've made the guacamole and red rice following his mother's special recipes, and made sure that we have fresh corn tortillas, heated just right. I even went over to Pottery Barn and bought perfect colorful Italian bowls. Teo picks up a bottle of tequila on his way home, and lavishes everyone with margaritas and Dos XX beer with lime and salt.*

After dinner we push the chairs out of the way, turn up the salsa and dance, with Teo pulling one delighted young woman after another out into the middle of the group for a turn as his partner. Dancing is one of his brightest talents and joys: he twirls, gyrates, dips and bends with fluid grace and a perfect sense of rhythm. I watch, trying not to feel jealous, as he turns the full force of his charm on one partner after another, leading each one masterfully through the steps. At last it is my turn and I laugh aloud as we move into the familiar patterns of salsa. I am so lucky to be married to this man, the one all my single women friends want to dance with.

Was it about this time that I began to feel like my head and my heart were running on parallel but entirely separate tracks? Intellectually, I was moving full steam ahead, finishing up my qualifying exams, trying to work out my dissertation topic, organizing a graduate student colloquium at NYU, beginning to send papers out to conferences and journals. I rarely talked about any of this with Teo, who did not read books or newspapers, and had no interest in the esoteric topics my grad school friends and I discussed. At home, I lived on a mundane, bodily plane: cooking, eating, making love, going out for walks in the city. I felt like I had the best of all worlds: I had all the intellectual stimulation I needed from school and my friends there, while the romance and passion Teo offered made me deeply happy at home.

Memories of graduate school

I have taken the train from Manhattan to New Haven to present my very first paper at an academic conference, the annual meeting of the American Comparative Literature Association, held that year at Yale. Before my panel begins, I panic and run to the ladies' room to gulp some Excedrin, hoping the hit of caffeine will enable me to focus and stop being distracted by my nerves. I get up before the packed audience at my panel, practically hyperventilating, and begin to read my paper with a cracked voice and shaky hands. I nearly cry with relief when it's over and I can sit down again, to polite applause. I am pleased and amazed to get some provocative questions from the audience during the Q&A–they were listening! They cared what I had to say! Suddenly my nerves abate and I feel like I'm entering a swift-running intellectual current that carries me forward easily. It's a welcome surprise to discover that I can swim.

I've been given the honor of developing and teaching my very own undergraduate class in Comparative Literature at NYU–not a section of expository writing, which I've been doing for a while already, but my very own literature class, which I call Modern Prose Styles. It's an exploration of different stylistic experiments by modernist European authors like Virginia Woolf, Franz Kafka, Henri Breton, and so on. I spend hours preparing my notes, carefully creating detailed class plans in which I ask a series of questions about the text, and build in answers based on close reading of passages I've not only already found, but typed in full into my notes. Nothing left to chance. I have the persistent nightmarish anxiety that if I don't write it all down in advance, I will find myself in front of the class gaping blankly, with nothing to say and no where to hide.

The first few weeks of the semester, when I show up for the class, I can feel my whole body shaking with excitement and nervousness, which fortunately falls away as soon as we get into the swing of the discussion and I pick up the engaged, passionate vibes of the students. It is such a surprise to find that I enjoy teaching; I, for whom speaking up in a college or graduate school class was always hugely nerve-wracking, complete with a shaking voice and shortness of breath. Somehow being the teacher creates a structure that enables me to manage my nerves: I prepare with elaborate care, and then once I'm in class I focus on facilitating the discussion, which leaves me no time to overthink and second-guess myself, my problem as a student. The stage fright I've had since my sixth grade trauma with "Fiddler on the Roof" begins to relinquish its stranglehold on me. I find myself looking forward to the two times a week when I will walk into the front of the room and call the class to order.

Walking down Greene Street after class with one of my grad school friends, Mary, our conversation grows heated as we air our complaints about our Comp Lit doctoral program. After a solid two years of doing little besides reading poststructuralist theorists like Derrida, Foucault, Barthes, Spivak, Kristeva, Benjamin, Lacan and so on and so forth, I am beginning to rebel. The hall-of-mirrors approach to politics is starting to seem sterile and unproductive. What good does it do anyone in the real world for me to spend hours and days unraveling the subversive tropology of XYZ canonical French novel? How is it possible that intellectuals this smart are advocating what is beginning to seem to me like a twisted form of mental masturbation? Mary *listens to me rant, and doesn't disagree; but like me, she is already too far down the Ph.D. path to turn off now. We throw our backpacks down in the comforting gloom of an East Village bar and order a first round of drinks, our intense dialogue succeeding, if nothing else, in letting off some steam.*

It's the fall of my first year of being ABD, all-but-dissertation, and I'm wandering restlessly around the streets of lower Manhattan, trying to think up a dissertation topic that will be more than just an academic exercise. How can I use my avocation of literature, and the poststructuralist tools I have been given in grad school, to make a positive difference in the real world? I poke my way into a cramped, stylish little bookstore on Spring Street in Soho and browse, conscious of the deep pleading of my heart for guidance. An hour later, I walk out clutching three books that seemed to have been placed there just for me to find: I, Rigoberta Menchú; Zami: A New Spelling of My Name *by Audre Lorde; and* Borderlands/La frontera, *by Gloria Anzaldúa. I carry the books back to my quiet apartment with a sense of excitement and immediately dive into them, a first reading that rocks my world and shocks me awake. Here is the in-your-face, no-holds-barred kind of writing and the radical political knowledge that I have been hungering for in grad school without even realizing what I was missing or being able to articulate what I wanted. I am catapulted into an entirely new, entirely unfamiliar intellectual space. But I know, with the same sense of certainty I had in moving from city to country in my childhood, that I belong not in the arid, patriarchal landscape of post-structuralism, but in this leafy, vibrant garden of electrifying words created by powerful women of color. I begin to quietly explore this new terrain, feeling like somewhat of a trespasser, but wanting desperately to be recognized and welcomed for the soul sister I feel I am.*

I felt an uncanny sense of connection with Lorde, Anzaldúa and Menchú right from the start. Their perspectives flooded my entire life experience with a new light. I marveled to learn that Lorde had grown up only blocks away from me in Manhattan, and had gone to the same high school as me, Hunter High— but her experience, as the daughter of Grenadian immigrants, was very different. Anzaldúa was at the center of the emerging "women of color" movement in New York and San Francisco in the early 1980s, and the way she fused political activism with indigenous spirituality was deeply moving and intriguing to me, suddenly opening up entirely new fields of inquiry. I was shocked at the brutality Menchú and her family faced at the hands of the colonizers, her testimonial rekindling my longstanding interest in Native peoples.

Reading about the barriers that centuries of racism had created for these women, it was as if a veil dropped from my eyes, enabling me to see my own privilege, as a well-educated white woman from a strong, supportive family, for the first time. I began to be able to frame my experiences in Mexico—where I had witnessed poor people, most of them of obvious indigenous heritage, being treated with such casual disregard—in light of the broader dynamics of power and privilege in the Americas, from colonial times to the present. Here, in my outrage over the oppressive dominant culture and my compassion for those resisting, was a place that my head and my heart could meet.

I am reading and re-reading I, Rigoberta Menchú, *the English translation of her testimonial, titled in Spanish* Me llamo Rigoberta Menchú y así me nació la consciencia *(My name is Rigoberta Menchu and this is how my political consciousness was born). As I read, I feel my own political consciousness developing; my learning curve is steep, as I begin to move beyond the textual politics I had played with for most of my graduate school career, into the flesh-and-blood, life-and-death politics of Menchú's world. She is only four years older than I am; but while I was growing up in a bright, sunny apartment on Park Avenue, she was growing up in a dirt-floor hut on a steep, cold mountainside in Guatemala, where her parents were trying to carve out a homestead—the indigenous people of Guatemala having long since been pushed out of the rich arable land down near the coast. Since they* could not subsist entirely on their own crops up on the mountain, Rigoberta's family had to go down to the coastal plantations to work for several months a year, transported by truck with other families.

Just as I spent my childhood going back and forth from Manhattan to upstate New York in my father's air-conditioned Buick, Rigoberta also spent her childhood going from a place she loved—the Altiplano, her mountainside home—to a place she hated, the plantations where she and her family worked. Sitting alone in my chic little apartment on Fifth Avenue, I weep with anger and sadness every time I read her description of that journey. She describes traveling for more than 24 hours in the enclosed cargo area of a dirty old truck; men, women and children crowded in the back with their dogs, cats and chickens. The drivers would stop to refresh themselves, but would not let the human cargo out, so they had to relieve themselves right there in the truck, like animals. "By the end of the journey the smell—the filth of people and animals—was unbearable," she said. "By the time we got to the finca, we were totally stupefied; we were like chickens coming out of a pot."

This description, along with so many other brutal tales from Menchú's experience, reminded me of the Holocaust stories I had read with such horrified fascination as a teenager: ordinary people being treated as if they were subhuman, one group of people being totally discriminated against by another, more powerful group. Menchú began her testimonial by reminding the reader that her story was not just her own—it was the story of her people, her entire generation. I sympathized instinctively with the friends and family she described, who were treated so harshly by the ruling Guatemalan elites. But as I read on in her account, I was forced to realize that I owed Rigoberta more than just sympathy, because as an American, I was complicit in the sufferings of her family and her people. The United States, just as it had during our own Indian wars, supported the racist, vicious plantation owners and other elites in their attempt to subjugate the Native people and take total control of the land.

I realized that what was being done to the indigenous people of Guatemala in the late 20th century was as wrong as what had been done, centuries earlier, to the Mohicans who were pushed out of the land that now belonged to my family. I had been born into this racist system; I had not created it, but I had, unconsciously, enjoyed and accepted it. Now, having become aware of it, I wanted to take a stand with my newfound teachers, these powerful women of color—a stand against racism, greed and exploitation. I would do it the only way I knew how, for the moment: with my writing. I wrote in my journal, in a firm, determined hand: "My name is Jennifer Browdy and this is how my political consciousness was born."

I am meeting with my academic advisor in his cramped office in the shabby NYU humanities building on University Place. He is listening to me quietly, patting some tobacco into his pipe, lighting it and taking a few puffs before responding to the dissertation plan I've just laid out so eagerly. I want to do a study of personal narratives by authors whose identities are culturally hybridized: Mexican-American, African-American, Native American, Asian American, in North America, Latin America and the Caribbean. I want to study the way these authors embed the broader cultural power dynamics into their own individual autobiographies. I'll start with my favorite authors—Audre Lorde, Gloria Anzaldúa and Rigoberta Menchú—and move on to cast a broader net as I develop the topic. My advisor, who specializes in 19th century French Romanticism, clears his throat and taps his pipe on the desk thoughtfully. Who will supervise this dissertation, he wonders? The topic seems very big and unwieldy—how will I compare texts from such a vast geographical and cultural range? What exactly do I mean by "hybrid subjectivity"? He smiles and pulls at his pipe again as I launch into my explanations, undaunted.

Stubbornly, I stuck to my vision, sharpening the proposal and buttressing it with a solid reading list of primary and secondary sources. I would be reading personal narratives in French, Spanish and English, all written by authors with "hyphenated," marginalized identities, people of color from the Americas: Latin America, the Caribbean and North America. There was nothing else in the world anyone could persuade me to focus on. With a sigh, my advisor acquiesced and agreed to supervise my dissertation, warning me that I'd be largely on my own since the topic was so foreign to him. I enlisted a Latin Americanist who had some interest in autobiography theory to be my second reader, and she drew in the third, drafting him on to my committee from the CUNY Graduate Center, since there was no one at NYU with the kind of knowledge I needed.

In 1991, when I began working on my dissertation, the fields of Ethnic Studies, African American Studies, Caribbean Studies and Women's Studies were still struggling to establish themselves as programs or departments within the universities. The culture wars of Allan Bloom and Dinesh D'Souza were raging full force, with a savage conservative backlash against the attempts to open the academic canon to more writers and thinkers from outside the white, Eurocentric mainstream. Like most women, I had never, in all my years of education, had the opportunity to take a course in women's studies, African American studies or feminist theory.

In my own instinctive, untutored way, I gravitated towards the voices that seemed the most compelling and meaningful to me, and once I had found them, I could not go back, even though much of what they said made me profoundly uncomfortable, sad and even, at times, frightened. I knew that the women warriors I was reading were the mentors I had been hungering for all my life. I wrote my way towards them with determination, hoping to one day prove myself worthy of their company.

But in the meantime, I continued to live a profoundly different kind of life. It was the kind of life where, for instance, Teo and I met my parents for a birthday dinner at Cellar in the Sky, the small glamorous restaurant up at the top of the World Trade Center, an exclusive enclave within the larger, more commercial (but still very fancy) Windows on the World restaurant. At Cellar in the Sky, there was a prix fixe menu of five courses, each one accompanied by the perfect fine wine. By the end of the meal we were all joyfully tipsy, superbly well fed, laughing and weaving our way down the super-fast elevators of the World Trade Center and out into the balmy air of a June evening, where we caught separate taxis home, my parents to 1185 Park, Teo and I to 24 Fifth. Another night, celebrating my birthday, we met up at Le Bernardin, the ravishing fish restaurant in midtown, where even the décor and furniture reeked of good fortune. My parents gave me a magnificent pearl necklace clasped with gold, gleaming royally in its black velvet carrying case. Teo gave me the pearl drop earrings I'd seen and coveted in a Madison Avenue jewelry store window. There seemed to be no limit to the good things around every corner of my life.

Teo and I have gone to visit his family in Mexico City, and now we're on a little getaway of our own, flying to Merida, renting a car, and driving down to Chichen Itza and the coast. At Chichen Itza, the power of the ruins awes and frightens me, especially the eerie, turquoise blue cenote—*a deep, open well—that I discover in a remote corner of the stone city. As I lean over the railing to look down into the water, there is a flash of orange-blue and I look up to see an exotic bird, which I'll later identify as a Quetzalcoatl, fly by. I am chilled when Teo tells me how this ceremonial* cenote *was used by the Mayan priests to discard the young human sacrifices they made to their gods.*

The next day we head down to the coast in our rental car, planning to find a place to stay near Tulum. On the way, we stop at another ruin, Coba, which the guidebook says is worth a look. An old man, dark and wrinkled, is waiting by the gate; he becomes our guide, leading us through ruins thickly overgrown with jungle. We climb to the top of a pyramid and look out over the forest; I have a deep sense of how insignificant we are compared to the great stone structures around us, no more or less than the dragonflies that dart around us in profusion. As we leave, our guide presses a big, round, shiny brown seed pod into my hands, smiling at me and speaking earnestly in a language I can't understand. I am moved and delighted by the gift, wishing I knew what kind of seed it was, and what it might grow into.

Teo and I rent a whitewashed bungalow right on the smooth, azure Caribbean sea, just a short distance from Tulum. I sink onto the bed with a feeling of rapture, and my whole body says YES when Teo takes me in his arms. After a while, he disappears for a moment, and returns quickly, beckoning me to come outside. In the dune right outside our cabin, he has prepared a little nest, laying a blanket over the sand and raising some protective walls around it. We make love passionately there, the sighing of the sea in our ears, with a new sense of intention: I have gone off the Pill for the first time since I was a teenager, and we are hoping now to conceive our first child.

The next thing I know, I am lying in bed in the little studio apartment at 24 Fifth Avenue, on a hot August afternoon. The air conditioner is grinding away; I feel nauseous and dizzy with a pounding headache. According to the home pregnancy test I took this morning, I am pregnant, a condition I had imagined would make me so happy! But now Teo is away at work, my parents and brother are off on a three-week trip through Alaska, and I am left home alone, too nauseous and weak to brave the heat to buy myself the one thing I am craving to eat—watermelon. I wish Teo would call to check on me, so I could ask him to bring home some groceries. But the phone doesn't ring. I am alone with my misery. I cry, feeling sorry for myself and, despite the new life pulsing in my belly, so very alone.

AIR

SWEPT AWAY

Looking back over the long trajectory of my education, from college through graduate school and into life as a professional academic, it disturbs me profoundly to realize how much I lost even as I gained the tools and trappings of that well-respected vocation, a professor of higher education. Although I chafed at the way my graduate education in comparative literature was largely divorced from real political awareness and efficacy, I went along with it: my Master's thesis was a marvel of post-structuralist jargon on a topic of purely academic interest; and although I tried to bring real people and politics into my dissertation, it was still written in the disembodied voice that I had been taught was the correct posture for a literary critic. Who I was as a person—what my life experience had been, and how that influenced the way I read texts (we never used the term "authors")—was considered irrelevant by my professors.

My dissertation, however, was a study of auto-biographies and personal narratives by writers like Audre Lorde and Gloria Anzaldúa, who insisted that quite the opposite was true: that it was essential to locate myself in my social and political context, to write out of, in Anzaldúa's words, "blood and pus and sweat"; that I should never allow "the master's tools," in Lorde's famous formulation, to silence my own authentic voice. For many years I held this disjunction uncomfortably within myself, knowing Lorde and Anzaldúa to be right, yet docilely continuing to write conventional literary criticism to appease the gatekeepers of Academia—the journal editors, the conference and curriculum review committees, the scholarly presses.

When I entered the artificial landscape of Academia, I left behind my dedication to my old childhood friends the maple trees and the chickadees. Living in Manhattan again for ten years between my graduation from college and the birth of my first child, I became a full-fledged city person, visiting the country on weekends with my parents, but without any of the old thrill that I used to get from being there. Like everyone else I knew, I was immersed in the daily striving for success: earning that Ph.D. with accolades from my professors and getting a teaching job; finding a life partner and getting married. Although my dissertation reading was beginning to teach me more about the larger political realities of my nation and the world, and although I still had the capacity to empathize deeply with the suffering of others, I was only just beginning to understand the bigger picture of how my own people, the American elite, were the force behind so much of the suffering, not only of people, but also of animals and the natural world.

In forgetting the joy and satiety I had known when I went on my long, solitary, meditative walks in the woods and fields as a child and adolescent; in allowing myself to be seduced by the glamour of conventional "success," I lost a vital source of spiritual energy—what Audre Lorde called "the erotic," defined as "self-connection shared," "the open and fearless underlining of [our] capacity for joy," "our most profoundly creative source" and "the nurturer...of all our deepest knowledge." The erotic, Lorde said, "is not a question only of what we do; it is a question of how acutely and fully we can feel in the doing." It is distinct from the pornographic, which, on the contrary, "emphasizes sensation without feeling."

As a child and adolescent, my relation to the natural world had been erotic in Lorde's sense. As I got older, I sought from human relationships the exhilaration, satisfaction and sense of total engagement and fulfillment that I used to get from roaming the mountainside at dawn, but I rarely found that depth of connection with other people. Sometimes in conversation with a kindred spirit; sometimes with a lover; but it wasn't often that I was able to reach down into the depths of my own passion, physical or intellectual, and share it with someone who was open to receiving what I had to give. There were many more times when I was disappointed in the shallowness of the people around me, or rebuffed by their confusion of the erotic with the pornographic.

Returning to Lorde and Anzaldúa now, at midlife, I find insights that I could not have understood when I first read their work in my twenties. Back then, I admired their outspokenness: their willingness to speak truth to power, to turn "the master's tools" back against the master and seek new ways to express knowledge that had been systematically suppressed by a society they were unafraid to call patriarchal. I admired their ability to get angry in print, and also to recognize that there are different types of anger, some destructive, some profoundly productive. As a young woman, I could admire Anzaldúa and Lorde and I could aspire to follow their lead, but I was still so bound by the self-imposed constraints of convention that my aspirations remained largely invisible to the outside world. I wanted to be married, to have a career, to have children, to be carried along comfortably by the stream of life. There's nothing wrong with any of this, except that the stream I chose moved me further and further away from the deepest core of my own passionate self, which was still out there in the woods with Estrella, trying to save the forest.

Audre Lorde described herself as coming out of her young adult years "blackened but whole," burnt by the racism and homophobia of the society into which she was born, cramped by poverty and lack of easy channels through which to send her brilliance out into the world. I had none of those challenges to deal with, sailing through my young adult years easily. It wasn't until I hit full adulthood, as a married working mother, that I began to feel the heat of fire—the element that will mold us, sometimes violently, into wiser beings, assuming we survive. Fire also lights our deepest passions, our inspiration to use our lives in positive service to the world. When I had my first son, at age 30, and my second son at 36, I threw myself wholeheartedly into mothering. It wasn't a conscious choice; it was the only way I knew how to relate to my beautiful babies, who called on me sweetly, lovingly, to give them everything I had to offer. In my relation with my children, at least, I felt the glimmerings of a return of the erotic energy I craved: the joy of "self-connection shared."

FIRE

FORGING A LIFE

I'm in the third trimester of my pregnancy, and I'm feeling big and beautiful, able to eat with gusto for the first time in a long time without worrying that I will "get fat." Teo and I have rented an apartment in a posh Westchester suburb of New York, but for the last couple of weeks of my pregnancy we stay at 1185 with my parents; I will be giving birth at one of the best hospitals in New York, under the care of my Park Avenue gynecologist. I face The Birth calmly, confident that I will once again be supported by my trusty red carpet.

I go into labor in the middle of the night on April 1, no fooling. In the morning, my dad and Teo get into their suits and ties and go off to work, leaving me in the kitchen with my mom. Under whatever strange pregnant lady's compulsion, I've asked my mom to make the filling for stuffed grape leaves, and I'm sitting in the kitchen, my great belly pressing up against the edge of the table, rolling grape leaves and breathing into the contractions. Around midday my mom finally prevails upon me and we take a yellow cab downtown to the hospital; it's the first time I've ever been there.

Having determined that I am sufficiently dilated, the nurses get me up on a gurney in one of the cold, blue-green labor rooms; I lie on my back, my belly strapped to a fetal monitor, waves of unbelievable pain flooding me as the contractions start. The woman OB-GYN I'd been seeing through my pregnancy does not show up; instead I get one of her partners, a male doctor I've never met before. He huddles in the door to my room talking with Teo, who eventually comes to tell me that the doctor has suggested I have an epidural for the pain. Although I had not wanted drugs, I quickly assent, and soon I'm watching the surging waves of contractions on the fetal monitor, without the slightest sensation in my body whatsoever. It's surreal.

Hours later, it's time to push. "Push, push! Push like you're really constipated!" the nurse urges me. I push, still on my back up on the narrow gurney, strapped to the fetal monitor. And then suddenly the nurse is telling me to stop pushing—the baby's head is crowning but the delivery room is not ready. Stop pushing—is she crazy? I can't stop pushing, I am caught up in the heaving paroxysms of birth now. They wheel me out into the hallway, still pushing, and finally I am in the delivery room, a big, shadowy, dark green room lit by a bare bulb. There is the snapping sound of scissors—an episiotomy, something else I hadn't wanted—and a sudden sense of total relief as my son slips into the air and starts bawling. I am breathless with happiness and the anticipation of holding him.

The nurse shows him to me, all wrapped up in a flannel blanket, and then suddenly he is gone. Teo tells me that they've taken him to the nursery, but I have to wait here on the delivery table until the anesthesiologist comes to sew up my episiotomy. We wait. We wait. I start to feel more and more deflated, like a piece of damaged meat on the table. I send Teo to go look for the baby, who has been taken to another floor. Finally the anesthesiologist arrives, a jaunty young man, who gives me an excruciatingly painful shot and starts sewing. When he's done, I'm moved to the recovery room, where it's determined that I can't feel my legs—and I can't be rejoined with my baby until I can feel my legs.

I lose it and start crying, waiting there on the bed in the big recovery ward with dozens of other patients recovering from all kinds of operations. I had never seen myself as "sick" during my pregnancy, other than those first miserable few weeks—but now I am classified as disabled, unable to feel my legs and thus unfit to hold my baby. I send Teo out again, desperate with worry about the baby, sure he is screaming for me—I still have not gotten to hold him for even a minute since he's been born!

It is two hours before I am allowed to move to my bed in the natal ward, and they finally bring me my baby. As I suspected, he is terribly upset. He has been screaming, the nurse tells me; so they decided to

*try giving him a bottle. I proffer my nipple, but he is
too upset to focus on it. All night he cries and I cry
with him. My poor baby! What have I done, entrust-
ing him and myself to this hospital, this doctor, this
system? It takes us many months to recover from this
trauma. Maybe we never do.*

We stayed with my parents at 1185 for the first
couple of weeks after the birth of our first son. I was
on a steep learning curve as far as mothering goes,
never even having held a baby until I had my own;
and every night, perhaps haunted by the trauma of
his birth, my infant cried hysterically from 11 p.m.
to 2 a.m., inconsolable. I held him miserably, feeling
inadequate and exhausted, until finally he fell asleep
and I could rejoin the rest of the sleeping household. During the day I took him out for walks in
his brand new Italian perambulator, following the
old routes along Park, Madison and Fifth Avenues
that I used to take with Pushkin. My mom gave me
pointers, held and played with the baby—she was
the first to get him to smile—and kept the delicious
meals coming. But eventually we had to go home to
our rented apartment in Westchester. And there the
loneliness of the new mother really set in.

*I am wheeling my baby along Main Street in Rye,
where we have rented our first apartment as a new
family of three. The street is lined with lush trees and
shiny red and black Mercedes and BMWs; expensive*

clothing and housewares are artfully laid out in the gleaming shop windows. In my jeans and sneakers, sans make-up or hairspray, I feel out of place and alienated; what am I doing here among all these society matrons? I don't know why I am so outraged when a powdered, be-ringed dowager, peering at my son curiously while we're waiting at the check-out line in the A&P, looks up at me to ask—clearly assuming that I'm the nanny—"Is he an Eskimo baby?"

In our apartment, a simple two-bedroom unit over the owner's garage, I try to concentrate on writing my dissertation during the baby's afternoon naps. I'm writing about power dynamics in hybrid ethnic identities of the Americas, as observed in writers like Audre Lorde, Gloria Anzaldúa, Richard Rodriguez, Leslie Marmon Silko and Rigoberta Menchú. But it's hard to focus, hard to remember why I was so passionately attracted to this topic in the first place. The alluring intellectual milieu of graduate school seems so far away as I go through my 1950s-style routine of taking care of my baby and shopping and cooking for my hubby, who takes the train home from Manhattan in time for dinner every day.

The baby is adorable, with his dancing brown eyes and chubby golden-toned face. I love him with a fierce passion, and yet there are many days when I sit with him in the rocking chair and just sob as though my heart is breaking. I have no friends out in the suburbs, and my city friends seem to have forgotten about me. I feel suddenly tossed up on shore away from the rushing *current of life, and I don't know how to get myself back into the game. I am happiest when I put my little Eskimo boy in the backpack and take him for long walks out in the marshlands by the coast, beyond the reach of the tangled web of social contradictions in which I find myself constantly struggling.*

In the fall of 1992, we decided not to sign another lease in Westchester. My parents had built a big house on their upstate property, and the little octagonal house was available. Teo was unhappy at his bank job, ready to try something new: he started a financial and legal translations business, working from home with clients in New York and Mexico. I was still working on my dissertation, and thrilled with the idea of moving to the country. Where better to raise my baby? Living in the little house again, I felt snug and embraced by its cedar and stone interior, enlivened by the windows looking out into the beloved woods and fields of my childhood. I was still lonely, but no longer alienated by my surroundings. By the spring of 1994, I was able to finish and defend my dissertation, earning the Ph.D. in Comparative Literature ten years after I'd entered graduate school.

As soon as my baby boy can walk, I begin introducing him to the woodland trails I've loved all my life, taking him to all my favorite haunts. We both love the rock-strewn, hemlock-lined trail running alongside a sparkling clear mountain stream, culminating in a dramatic waterfall that splits over a jutting boulder I privately call "Indian Heart," because it looks like a heart to me and I know that it must have been a sacred stone for the Mohicans who once loved this land.

One spring day we venture up higher, going by car up to the peak of the mountain along whose flank the Indian Heart stream meanders. When my parents took me up to the top of this mountain as a child to pick wild blueberries, the rugged landscape always reminded me of the illustrations in the book Blueberries for Sal: broad slabs of rock somewhat softened by the clustered blueberry bushes and the stunted, wind-gnarled pine trees. Only the toughest grasses and lichens can survive up here. While my little boy leaps from rock to rock playing his own imaginary games, I sit still in the center of a giant flattened boulder, tapping into the immense sleeping power of the mountain beneath me and the broad, limitless sky overhead. The view, across valleys and distant mountain chains, pulls my gaze outward, but I feel somehow collected and focused, too, as if I am sitting in the center of an energy vortex that is using me as a link for earth and sky, past and present.

It comes to me that another woman has sat in this same place, long ago in human terms, but just an instant ago in mountain-time reckoning. I know that she was a seer; she made the journey up to the top *of the mountain on foot, by herself, purifying herself along the way in the cold stream, preparing herself to do the sacred work of aligning her human consciousness with the Great Spirit of earth and sky to bring back new knowledge to guide her people. The visions she received up here were not good. Sitting for several days and nights, through a wild thunderstorm and the cool rainbows that followed, she began to smell the foul odor of unwashed sailors in their wooden ship, making their way up the river that would come to bear the name of their captain, Henry Hudson. She was frightened by the sense of foreboding that overtook her as the vision deepened. The scream of a hawk wheeling overhead brought her out of her trance, as it brings me out of mine. The question for her, as for me, is urgent but so hard to answer: what should we do with the knowledge and awareness we have been given?*

Since having my consciousness raised about indigenous history in the Americas, I had begun an interdisciplinary self-education in Native American studies, with a special focus on Native American women and the connections between indigenous cultures throughout the Americas. It was painful yet inspiring reading: painful because the histories of brutal displacement, extermination and dehumanization were so full of despair, but inspiring because despite it all, the indigenous women writers I admired were defiantly, proudly, fiercely alive, telling their stories to honor those lost as well as the survivors who refused to be vanquished.

Traveling this historical trail of tears, I began to be aware of ghostly voices at every turn, lamenting over the injustices that had been visited upon them. I came to understand that the only difference between my seemingly peaceful corner of North America and Rigoberta Menchú's violent Central American homeland was that in my region the native peoples had been displaced centuries ago, while in Guatemala and other parts of Central and South America they had survived the initial colonial onslaught and were still trying to live on their ancestral lands, keeping their ancient cultures, languages and customs alive—in particular, their reverence for the natural world.

The tough question I began to ask myself was: What difference was there between me and a Guatemalan landowner—weren't we both thieves? Maybe I wasn't directly involved in exploiting the Indian families who labored on the coastal plantations, but I sure was happy to drink that coffee and flaunt that inexpensive new cotton shirt, wasn't I? And I had no compunction whatsoever about claiming ownership rights over that beautiful piece of land I called home. But what had happened to the Native peoples who used to live on and love this land?

Menchú's story made me see myself as an American of European descent in a whole new—and not at all positive—way. Yes, most of my ancestors had come to America fleeing the pogroms and persecution back in the nightmarish Jewish Pale of Russia and Poland. But as soon as they got off the boat at Ellis Island, they began to benefit from being white-skinned in a racist society. My family had also benefited, like generations of European immigrants before us, from the clearing of the land of its indigenous people and the new system of property ownership that allowed my grandparents to buy a deed to land that had no doubt been stolen or swindled from the Mohican people a couple of centuries earlier.

In the 1990s, some progressive African American and Native American leaders were calling for reparations—cash payments to compensate the descendants of those who had been enslaved, displaced and discriminated against. This seemed just to me, though it did not gain much traction—the immensity of what had been lost made the idea of a reasonable, ethical recompense remote. Watching my son run around the woods and fields of our lovely home, I mused to myself: what would I think if a Mohican turned up with an ancient claim on this land? How far would my newfound sense of justice go?

I had already begun to work through these questions in my dissertation, the first chapter of which became one of my first published essays, "Of Tortillas and Texts," about the shaky alliance between testifier and scribe in Rigoberta Menchú's testimonial. Although the scribe, Venezuelan journalist Elisabeth Burgos-Debray, presented herself as an ally to Menchú, it was a flawed model of alliance across culture and class, because Burgos did not treat Menchú as a full partner in the book they produced together.

On the positive side, *I, Rigoberta Menchú* became an international bestseller, translated into many languages and selling more than a million copies. The work Menchú and Burgos did together helped shine an international spotlight on the social, environmental and economic injustices being perpetrated on the indigenous peoples of Central and Latin America, and made it more difficult for American and European countries to collaborate with impunity with the local oppressors. The testimonial was widely read in colleges and universities throughout the world, changing the way privileged young people like me viewed the previously almost invisible poor folk of the world.

But Burgos retained the copyright and did not give Menchú a fair share of the royalties. In her later book, *Crossing Borders*, Menchú dreamed sadly of recovering the rights to her own story, and spoke acidly of scholars like Burgos: "People make careers out of us, people think they can live by studying other human beings...We create defenses against these parasites. Getting to know another culture is wonderful but it is ignoble when certain irresponsible individuals try to put human dignity in a bottle and make a profit from selling it."

The last thing I wanted was to be a parasite like this. I wanted to earn the respect of people like Rigoberta Menchú, to work alongside them in the struggle for social and environmental justice. But I wasn't quite sure how to do it. I couldn't imagine myself following the Che Guevara model and abandoning my comfortable life to slog through the jungle. Was it possible for a privileged person like me to collaborate successfully with someone from a very different background? What common ground could we meet on? How could we bridge the cultural gulf between us to work together towards common goals?

It is January 2, 1994, and I am boarding a plane in Mexico City to fly back home. We've been visiting with Teo's family for a week, and it's been somewhat trying—a constant party of rum-and-cokes and visiting relatives for Teo, a lot of running around after our lively toddler for me. I grab one of the free newspapers they're handing out at the door of the plane, and as we settle into our seats we are both shocked to see the headline: Indigenous Uprising in Chiapas; City of San Cristobal Taken. *What??! NAFTA, the North American Free Trade Agreement, had just gone into effect on January 1, and Teo's father, like many other middle-class Mexicans, had been hopeful that it would mean increased chances for business across the border. Teo's financial and legal translation business was already booming in anticipation of the new, more open business climate. What is going on in Chiapas?*

It pains me to recall how naïve I was about the realities of politics on the American continent. In 1994, I was only just beginning to read Margaret Randall, Noam Chomsky, and Eduardo Galeano, all of whom knew from the get-go that NAFTA would be a disaster for the poor of Latin America, while scoring another bonanza for the elites. Back home in snowy New York, I fell under the spell of Subcomandante Marcos, following him in the news as best as I could—the advent of the World Wide Web still a year or so away. In Marcos I recognized an intellectual like me, but one who had chosen to follow his moral compass right into the jungle, to live and struggle alongside the indigenous people he admired and wanted to help.

Looking over my shoulder at the pictures of the masked Marcos with his weapon over his shoulder and his pipe dangling from his lips, Teo snorted in disgust. To him, Marcos was a crazy dreamer who was going to wind up dead or in prison any day now. Progress was progress. The *indios* of Chiapas had to conform or get out of the way. Like most Mexicans I'd met, Teo could with one breath sing the praises of historical Aztecs like Cuauhtemoc or heroes of the Mexican Revolution like Pancho Villa, while in the next breath disparaging the contemporary indigenous people and *campesinos* of Mexico as backward and dumb. I had found out by this time that it was not worth trying to argue with him. What was the point, especially when it was true, as Teo liked to remind me, that much of our current income came from the big multinational corporations that were aggressively moving into the newly opened Mexican market? Just how hypocritical could I stand to be?

Nervously, I thread my way through the crowded hotel and convention center to the hushed upstairs corridor where I have an interview date with a university search committee. With my new Ph.D. in hand, I had applied for 10 positions from the Modern Language Association job list, and to my surprise I have gotten seven requests for interviews, all to be held at the MLA Convention in San Diego. Some of the interviews take place in the huge, noisy ballroom, a meat market for literature scholars, where the strained, exhausted demeanors of the interviewers make it hard to muster much enthusiasm for the position they are offering.

For this interview, however, I've been summoned to the university's elegant hotel suite, and this is the job I am most interested in. I can feel my heart thumping as I knock and enter the room, and when I speak I know my voice sounds tight and breathless. The four professors in the room interview me politely. But thinking back on it later, I realize that the whole thing was a charade from the moment they looked up at me expectantly as I entered the room, and I saw the disappointment register in their eyes before they recovered their composure. With a dissertation title of Hybrid

Encounters *and a Hispanic surname, they had been expecting a bonafide Latina to diversify their ranks. I'm not what they're looking for, no matter how eloquently I answer their questions.*

The truth was, I was not all that interested in stepping on to the tenure track just then, especially not if it would entail a major move to another region of the country. Teo was excited at the idea of moving, finding our new life in the country dull and the close proximity to my parents stifling. But I loved it. I loved living right next to my parents, being able to drop in on them and receive the encouragement, warmth and good meals that they always provided. I found it hard to imagine how I would manage with a demanding fulltime job—would I be willing to leave my baby in daycare from dawn to dusk? Would Teo step up and help out more in the house? The more I thought about moving to take a distant tenure-track job, the less I liked the idea, especially since I knew I wanted to have a second child sometime soon.

Thinking I'd just try to keep my hand in teaching while my main focus was on parenting, I paid a visit to the dean of a small nearby college, who welcomed me enthusiastically and threw me into teaching women's studies, general education and literature courses as an adjunct professor. I quickly settled into a busy routine of parenting and teaching, while Teo spent most of his time closeted in his office in town, making a living word by translated word. Our son started kindergarten in the sunny, warm atmosphere of a local Waldorf school. Life went on.

With my second pregnancy, I go into labor around midnight and the contractions speed up quickly. My mom comes over to sleep with our older son and Teo and I head out for the hospital, my overnight bag in the back seat. This time I have been much more careful; I have a midwife and a doula attending my birth, with the OB-GYN just on call as a backup if there are any problems. The hospital has a brand-new maternity wing; I have a private room with a bathroom, and I am not strapped down to a fetal monitor. I pace around, squat and push, and the doula rubs my back while the midwife puts warm oil around my vaginal opening—no episiotomy this time! In six hours, with remarkably little pain, my baby boy comes slithering out. He's wiped off and immediately placed on my chest, where he snuggles up to my breast, looking peaceful and a little dazed. Within minutes he is suckling contentedly and I am gazing down at him through eyes misting with love. My baby.

Perhaps because of his easy birth, our second son was a much more relaxed baby than the first, sweet-tempered and agreeable. And I was much more relaxed as a mother by then, too. With my older son, I had tried to listen to the experts who warned against letting your baby sleep in bed with you. With the new baby, I followed my own instincts; for most of his infancy he slept right on my stomach, where he could reach over to nurse without either of us having to fully wake up, much less get out of bed. A well-rested mother is a happy mother...and a happy mother makes for a happy baby. I took off a semester from teaching, and the boys and I had fun, going for hikes with the baby in the back carrier, carving pumpkins at Halloween, sharing a big Thanksgiving as usual with my parents, my brother and his family.

But there were a few moments from that year that I remember just as vividly, which remind me that underneath this peaceful surface, things were not so perfect.

I am holding the baby on my lap on the couch, facing me. He's about three months old now and can hold up his head pretty well, and I remember that when his brother was this age, he started to smile and giggle whenever an adult held him and talked to him cheerfully. But as much as I talk and coo, trying to get his attention, he doesn't seem to warm up. He looks past me, rather than into my eyes, and his expression remains blank. It's worrisome, especially with all the news lately about autism. Oh God no, not my baby!

A few months later, to my great relief, my baby boy has started smiling and interacting normally. One night, the four of us are eating dinner and at the same time, Teo and I are having an argument. I look at my children and know I should put a lid on it and not rise to whatever gauntlet Teo has just thrown across the table at me, but suddenly I see red—I can't control myself, and I snap back at him. Teo never, ever backs down from an argument. He has only one speed when it comes to a fight: forward, full throttle, escalating until the opponent backs down. I am his always-available opponent, and I always back down.

But on this evening I return his jabs a few times before subsiding into my usual state of simmering low-level resentment and anger. Our little kitchen is suddenly filled with harsh, angry tones and tension thick enough to slice. Our six-year-old son bows his head over his plate, trying to make himself invisible. I notice that the baby's round, cherubic face looks absolutely stricken and shocked. This is the first time he's been so close to discord, and there is a bewildered, frightened look in his eyes that I can only interpret as: Have I come to the wrong household? Instantly I drop my side of the battle. "Hablamos más tarde," I mutter to Teo, nodding meaningfully at the children. He glares at me but turns back to his plate. I hastily start talking cheerfully with the baby, trying to distract him with a new food to try. Feeling so guilty at exposing him to the rawness of conflict and anger, I swear to myself I will never let this happen again.

When I try to remember what we were fighting about in those days, the details don't come, but the general drift was always the same. His complaints: I did not appreciate him enough; I was too bossy; I was too involved with my parents; I was not active enough in bed. My complaints: he was not engaged enough in the childcare and housework, expecting me to do it all and also work for money and have energy left over to please him in bed. He also rarely made himself available for the family hikes and outings I loved to take with the boys. Ours was far from the kind of partnership I had imagined marriage to be; far from what I saw in my parents' marriage, which, though it did have strictly defined gender roles, was based in respect and trust and shared pleasures. As time went on, it became obvious that Teo and I had few shared pleasures. He liked dancing and going to clubs, which we never did once we moved upstate; I liked camping and hiking, which he had no interest in. In the early years of our romance I had loved to listen to him play guitar and sing, and I had shared my own repertoire of my father's folksongs with him. But after we moved to the country, he found other people to play with; he made fun of my quiet singing and playing, so I only played for the boys when he was not in the house. More and more, it became clear that the only thing keeping us together was our shared interest in raising our children. And even that was a source of argument, as he scoffed at the spiritual, nature-based Waldorf philosophy, which I loved wholeheartedly.

I never seriously considered leaving him, even when he would regularly snarl, in the course of our arguments, "Do you want me to leave? I'll pack up right now! Do you want me to go?" Though sometimes I would hear my heart saying, "Yes, please go," I always listened to my head, which said fearfully, "How will you manage on your own with the boys?" And so I turned my attention elsewhere as much as possible, and let the relationship ride. There were so many other things to be concerned about, after all.

It has been snowing hard all day, and I'm worried, pacing round and round the little house. The baby, now 8 months old, has a cold and the cough is sounding worse and worse. Finally he's standing up in his crib looking at me with a kind of desperation as he gasps for breath, the coughs sounding tight and deep within his chest. My mom comes over to check on us, and she is definite: he has to go to the doctor, NOW. But it's snowing so hard, I am worried about the drive over to the doctor's office. I call Teo, who comes home quickly from his office in town; we bundle the baby up and make the treacherous drive. It turns out to have been the right thing to do. The doctor immediately calls the hospital and arranges for the baby to be admitted. He has pneumonia and asthma.

At the hospital, they set up an oxygen tent over a crib, and my little boy lies there breathing painfully, looking scared and resigned. Teo goes back home while I stay overnight in the hospital, beside myself with worry. After two days in the hospital, we are discharged to begin our new regimen, picking up a nebulizer and steroid asthma meds on the way home. Our patient, cooperative baby will have to lie down inhaling cool vaporized medication four times a day, for twenty minutes a session. Instantly our lives are changed as we begin to adapt to this constraining routine. It's no fun at all.

We had to carry the nebulizer around with us everywhere for the next year. Eventually the medication dose was lowered to just morning and night, but there were a few more scares along the way, like the time when our little boy had to go in to the hospital for a chest x-ray, and he was crazed with fear when they wouldn't let us come with him into the darkened x-ray room. After that episode we noticed that he began to stutter, and for the next few years, whenever he was anxious or stressed, the stutter would come back. He also developed the same kind of crushing anxiety that I remembered from my own childhood, when I used to worry that something would happen to my mother. He couldn't explain what he was worried about, but his anxiety would sometimes reduce him to quivering, sobbing hysteria. He would clutch his stuffed Froggie, his beloved security animal, and moan, "I'm worried, Mommy! I'm worried!" before dissolving into tears. I hugged him and comforted him as best I could, but the worries always came back.

One spring day when he was about seven, still tormented at times by the anxiety that burst out of him in a persistent facial tic and stutter, I had the idea to take him on a ritual journey up the mountain and throw his worries off the cliff. He looked at me doubtfully when I explained what we were going to do, but he was always game for a hike, so we set off in the clear March sunlight. When we reached the summit of the mountain, high up on eye level with the wheeling hawks, we began looking for small stones to throw.

"Each stone will be one of your worries," I told him. "We're just going to throw them AWAY!" I pitched a stone off the side of the mountain, hard, and we smiled at each other as we heard it bounce satisfyingly, far below.

Handing me his Froggie, my little boy entered into the task with a will, throwing small rocks off the mountain as hard as he could. Eventually, his energy spent, he came to sit beside me on a big boulder, and we stared in companionable silence across the treetops at the blue mountains on the horizon. For the moment, at least, his mood had lifted, his face serene and content. It was a moment to hold on to.

It's a glorious fall day and I'm taking a walk with a friend, telling her about the new class I'm teaching on women's writing from Latin America and the Caribbean. "Last week, a student asked me, 'Why do you like to teach such depressing books?' and I didn't know how to answer her. Sometimes I feel badly that I'm making the students read such traumatic stories. I don't really know why I'm so drawn to stories of suffering, but I am," I say, musingly.

My friend, a therapist by trade, looks at me and comes out with one of her characteristic wise comments. "Rumi says that 'the wound is the place where the light enters you.' You are leading students through those wounded places in order to get at the light that can only be found there, on the other side of the pain," she says. I nod, pondering this. For me, these women writers' stories of suffering, courage and resistance are so inspiring and moving that increasingly they are the only types of narratives I am interested in studying in my classes and scholarly writing. Although the experiences of these politically active Latin American and Caribbean women writers are so different than anything I or my students have encountered in our privileged late 20th century North American lives, I know, without being able to put my finger on it, that there is something important we need to learn from them; a necessary clarity of vision that can only be found by accompanying them on their journeys through trauma and suffering.

Slowly I began to take a more overtly political stance in my teaching, writing and event organizing, but for the most part I left my progressive politics at the door when I came home. Teo had no interest in talking about politics, beyond expressing his distrust and disgust with all politicians. My parents might talk with engagement about American politics, but rarely got involved in Latin American issues, much less women's human rights.

I remember one day I was having lunch with my parents and a friend of ours, a woman who was a high-powered financier from a privileged background. Over an elegant lunch of imported cheeses, prosciutto, salad and wine, I launched into an impassioned speech about poverty and the exploitation of the poor by the wealthy, and how the corporate elites were working hand in hand with governments around the world to squeeze the maximum profits out of the environment and the people on the lowest rungs of the social ladder. It wasn't right, I argued, that the top 1% of society enjoyed fabulous wealth, while the bottom 50% lived in abject poverty. Why should this be so?

My parents were nodding in what could be interpreted as agreement, though they were not taking up the argument themselves, and were no doubt hoping I would say my piece and then yield, letting the conversation take a more desultory path. Our friend, who had been quiet until then, looked up at me and said in a matter-of-fact tone, all cool reason to my passionate bluster, "There have always been poor people in the world, and there always will be. There's really nothing to be done about it."

This blunt statement took the wind out of my sails, and haunted me for a long time afterward.

She was putting into words what might be called the "privilege principle," the psychological mechanism by which privileged people are able to see suffering, shrug, turn away and go on with our comfortable lives. I knew this stance well; I had grown up with it myself. I could not explain why it was that I began to see suffering and want to do something about it, while so many others I knew continued to live by the privilege principle and ignore it. I wasn't about to give up my privileged lifestyle, but I refused to simply accept things as they were, as if my own good fortune were some kind of manifest destiny. The more I learned about how very differently the other two-thirds of the planet's population lived, the harder it became to enjoy my still-unfurling red carpet ride.

It is September 12, 2001, a beautiful fall day, and Teo and I are taking the boys for a walk around a peaceful lakeside trail. We are still reeling from the shock of yesterday's attack on the World Trade Center. In my fear and grief I need to come out to the forest, and uncharacteristically, Teo consents to come along too. No airplanes are flying today, and suddenly their absence is palpable; the quiet is eerie. I feel like I'm in a kind of dream, the warm sunshine glinting on the clear blue lake, bird calls ringing out cheerfully, the boys running happily along the woodsy trail, completely innocent of knowledge of what has just happened (thankfully, we follow the Waldorf creed of no TV in the house), and me seeing all this through a dark veil of shock, grief and fear, wondering what will come next.

We sit down on the rocks at one end of the lake, and while the boys throw pebbles I am surprised and comforted to feel Teo slip his hand into mine. He regards public displays of affection disdainfully, and is proud, he says, that he and I don't need to show our love by holding hands or putting an arm around each other, much less kissing in public. But lately his public coolness doesn't warm up much when we're alone, either, and his simple gesture brings me nearly to tears. It is such a relief to feel the human contact, like rain after a long drought. I know it won't last long.

How does one recount the long slow failure of a marriage? There is no single cause or turning point, nor is there any use in blame. Like every lasting human relationship, a marriage is made hour by hour, day by day, in a constant stream of interactions, many of them unconscious and unintentional. When I married Teo, I was seduced by his passionate lovemaking and his exotic charm. I knew he was the product of an unrepentant macho culture, but I thought he would adapt to my liberal American world view. I knew he was a city boy, but I thought he would come to love and appreciate the starry skies and forested hillsides of rural New England. I knew he liked to drink and party, but I thought he would mature into a solid family man who preferred to spend time with his family. So much for wishful thinking.

In my married life, I was often reminded of a Mexican saying I had learned from Teo's mother: "*Luz en la calle, oscuridad en su casa*": "light in the street, darkness at home." She had used this saying to describe her own husband, who, like his son, was always charming and genial in public settings, but often irritable and remote at home. Teo, who was close to his mother, had resented his father for the way he treated her as little more than his housekeeper. Strange that he did not see, ten or fifteen years into our marriage, how he began to fall into just the same pattern with me.

How disappointed I was when he ignored my suggestions that we do something special, just the two of us, to celebrate our 10th anniversary, or our 15th! Years passed without our going out together on any kind of "date," unaccompanied by our children. We worked; we parented; we got up and did it all over again. We maintained a façade of cool affability in public, but the emotional distance between us grew. Not knowing how to rekindle our connection, I turned my focus outward and put my energy into mothering my sons, teaching my classes, and writing.

These were the years when I edited and published two anthologies of "women writing resistance," collecting hard-hitting contemporary writing by women from Africa, Latin America and the Caribbean. I also worked with a friend on a historical fiction about the fearsome 18th century women pirates Anne Bonny and Mary Read, who cross-dressed and crossed swords with some of the toughest men of their time, earning the respect of all the pirates they met. Casting my imagination back to this freer, wilder time, I was fascinated and inspired by the way Anne and Mary thumbed their noses at power and did exactly what they wanted. I wished I could be as bold in my own sphere.

It's a gloomy December day, the landscape grey with snow spitting fitfully from the sky. I am re-reading Dostoyevsky's novella Notes from Underground, *one of the required texts in the core curriculum seminar I've been teaching for more than a decade as an adjunct professor. I'm feeling grumpy about having to read it again; it's so depressing, and what does it add to the students' education, really, to focus on this pathetic narrator with his unhealthy obsession with chorus girls?*

My mind wanders to a recent faculty meeting, at which I and a couple of the younger faculty had tried yet again to get the senior faculty to consider opening up the curriculum to more women authors and writers of color, more voices beyond the traditional European canon. The discussion had been heated, with one of the older men finally throwing out the argument that it was perfectly fine that two of the four texts in the first semester were Greek, because after all, "the Greeks are a minority in Europe, aren't they?"

I'm infuriated by his willful refusal to recognize the narrow Euro-centrism of our canon, and incredulous that none of the other senior faculty see a problem with the fact that of the sixteen books in the required curriculum, only two are by women—Jane Austen and Virginia Woolf—and only one by a person of color, Frederick Douglass.

As I follow Dostoevsky's resentful hero down into his bitter underground lair, I have to smile, recognizing my own disgruntled resentment of my colleagues as comparable to his. Unable to compete with his rival, a handsomer and more powerful officer, he retreats underground to brood and stew and plot his revenge. Isn't that what I am doing too? With a sense of guilty pleasure, I begin to map out a parody of Notes from Underground, *based on my experience as an adjunct professor. I'll put in all the colleagues who have made my life difficult, thinly disguising the college itself to make it a* roman à clef. *In fiction I'll have the satisfaction of portraying them as the complacent conservatives I feel they are, and I'll be able to make myself a much braver and more dashing heroine than I've been able to pull off in real life. I'll show them!*

I never did write Notes from the Adjunct Underground, partly because right when I hit bottom, things finally started to improve. By dint of some determined strategic organizing with other colleagues, mostly women, I eventually got myself off the adjunct track at the college, succeeding in negotiating a longer-term contract, a decent 12-month salary, access to health insurance and other benefits. At the same time, a friend offered me a helping hand on to the faculty of an interdisciplinary program at a nearby state university and I began what would be my pattern for nine years: team-teaching 80 students per year at the university, while also teaching two classes a semester at the small college I continued to think of as my "home" institution. The university job paid well by academic standards—I was a lecturer, not an adjunct, so I was a union member with benefits and a salary set by agreement with the state—and it was enjoyable work. But the two part-time teaching jobs added up to much more work than a regular fulltime position, and of course I was still as dedicated as ever to keeping the home fires burning. I was kept constantly on the run, trying my best to do it all.

When I first started teaching part-time, while I had my babies, I had naively expected that I would easily be able return to the academic tenure track when I was ready. Slowly I realized that by stepping on to the so-called "mommy track" I had unknowingly dealt my career a serious blow, from which it would prove very difficult to recover. It was many years before I fully understood what so many feminists before me had found out: that women who prioritize parenting over a rapid climb of the career ladder—women who focus on so-called "marginal" works, rather than the old-boy canon—women who obey the social conditioning that enjoins us to *be polite and ask nicely*—well it's just too bad, but nice women like us are going to be kept firmly in our place, doing the dishes rather than sitting at the table, and expected to be grateful for whatever crumbs came our way.

Meanwhile, as the first decade of the 21st century advanced, I felt like I was constantly walking on thin ice at home, trying to hide my misery from my parents and to shield the boys from the fallout of their father's rage, which got harder and harder to do, as his bad temper frequently erupted in front of them. Any little irritation—say, my daring to ask for more of his help with childcare, as my paid workload increased—was the excuse for an immediate escalation: "I am the way I am, and I'm not going to change," he'd declare. "If you don't like me as I am, I'll leave. Do you want me to leave? I'm going to pack my bags right now!" he'd shout, and I'd back down silently, remembering how my mother used to tell me, "You marry to love someone, not to change them...." But the man I'd fallen in love with was not the man I now found myself married to.

Still, even as Teo's bitterness solidified into a stance of permanent negativity, evidenced by the deep furrow that knotted his brow when he was home, I refused to seriously consider that our marriage might be over. I had married him; he was the father of my children; I had to make the best of the life we had forged together.

It is about 9 p.m. on an August night, the quiet country landscape pulsating with crickets and softly lit by stars. The boys are in bed; Teo and I are puttering about the house. Suddenly we hear the deep roar of a truck making its way up our driveway. We look at each other, surprised; who would be coming up the driveway in a truck at this time of night? The truck goes past our house up towards the back of the property, and I figure the driver, lost, will turn around up there and go on his way. A few minutes later, we start to hear the sound of snapping trees and spinning wheels, followed by the slam of a door and a shouted expletive in the dark. "I'll go see what's going on," Teo says with agitation, and storms out into the darkness. I can tell by his tone that he's looking for a fight, and I look out the window fearfully.

Sure enough, within minutes I can hear the two men shouting at each other, each exchange punctuated by curses. I'm instantly worried: What if this guy has a gun? Who knows how this could end? Frantic and trembling, I pick up the phone and call 911. As I give the dispatcher our location and explain what's going on, I hear my mother coming down the driveway, and now I'm worried for her too—why is she going to get in the middle of these crazy men?

But it turns out that she knows why the guy with the truck is here. He is a contractor and she was expecting him; he just got his trailer stuck in the woods, as Teo might have found out if he'd gone out to help rather than to attack. It's too late though:

*the state trooper arrives, and things get worse. The
truck driver disappears quietly into his truck, and
the tall, tough trooper takes my Mexican husband
for the problem.*

*"Do you know this man?" he demands of my
mom. There is just a split second of hesitation before
she says yes and begins the process of explaining to the
trooper that the call had been a mistake, that there
was no problem, that he could leave. That hesitation
is enough to send Teo over the edge.*

*"Your mother was defending that truck driver over
me!" he rages after it's all over. "That's it. I'm leaving.
You can come with me or not, but I will not live here
with your parents any longer."*

I thought about just letting him go. But I was still
hopeful that perhaps if we were living in our own
house, away from my family, he would feel happier
and our home life would improve. I decided to move
with him, and within a month he had found us a
house to rent. It was hard to tear myself away from
the sheltering contours of our home, where every
slope of land, every rock outcropping and tree was
familiar to me since childhood, and so beloved. But
we were not moving far, and it was true that we had
outgrown the little house. It would be good to live in
a place where each boy could have his own bedroom,
I told myself, and there was an attic, a basement
and plenty of closets for all our stuff. Plus, I really
liked the house Teo had found. It was on a quiet

corner and the backyard faced into an undeveloped piece of maple woods. It had a deck with a grapevine growing on it, a peach tree, a raised vegetable bed, and a covered front porch overlooking a big, overgrown, intriguing perennial garden. On the golden September day when we went to take a look at it for the first time, I felt with certainty that the wheel of my life was turning again, but that it was for the best. This move would be a positive thing, I was sure.

So we went. The boys were thrilled to spread out in the new house, and Teo did seem happier, but he still refused to reconcile with my parents. When his parents came up to the U.S. on a rare visit, it was awkward because Teo did not want them socializing with my parents, even though, despite a serious language barrier, both sets of in-laws had always had an amicable relationship. I knew there was no point in arguing with him about it, and could not explain to my mother or my mother-in-law why Teo was behaving so strangely. After his parents left, I suggested, for the umpteenth time, that Teo consider talking with a therapist, or that we go for marriage counseling together, and for the umpteenth time he dismissed the idea. He didn't have a problem—everyone else was the problem. Right.

After the devastating second-term re-election of George W. Bush, my parents are spooked and decide to buy land in Canada, to have a place to run to if things become too nasty in the U.S. Before we know it they have bought a beautiful piece of land on an island in Nova Scotia, and built a big, comfortable new house. This summer Teo and the boys and I are staying in the house for two weeks, most of it by ourselves since things are still so tense between my parents and Teo. I am flabbergasted to see Teo sit, hour after hour, with his back to the beautiful view, reading first one John Grisham novel, then another. He's only interested in going to the beach to jog; the few times he does accompany us to sit on the beach on a sunny afternoon, he sits on his chair, under the umbrella, with his shoes still on. He insists that he doesn't like Nova Scotia because the water is cold and there's nothing to do; when I suggest we drive around and do some sightseeing, he's not interested in that either.

The boys swim and build sand castles and snorkel around the rocks, holding up wriggling crabs in delight. I give up on trying to get any warmth out of Teo, and retreat into cooking, reading and walking on the beach. I am not feeling so well; I have a hacking cough that I can't seem to shake. It gets worse when I sit on the beach with the cold wind blowing on me, and as we head home in the car it becomes so convulsive I feel like I can barely breathe. A bit of random French keeps coming back to me as I cough and cough all the way back to New England, Teo driving the car silent and remote beside me: "Je m'etouffe. Je m'etouffe!"

It turned out I had asthma; a fitting somatic manifestation of the way I was feeling suffocated in my marriage. Still, I made no move to change things. When I look back on this period, I find it hard to understand what kept me frozen in that unhappy marriage so long. Why didn't I have the courage and resourcefulness to make a move? What was I afraid of?

I was afraid of the financial repercussions of leaving him, even though I knew this to be irrational: by this point, with my two jobs, I was bringing home most of the bacon, and I knew I could count on my parents' support in an emergency.

I was somewhat afraid of *what people would think.*

But even more than that, I was wedded to my own self-image as a happily married wife and mother. Being a single mother was a whole different story, one I had never imagined or prepared myself for. It was not the story I wanted to be living.

In the face of my stubbornness, it was Teo who eventually made the first move to end our marriage.

This summer, Teo has decided he's not going to come along on our annual family vacation to Nova Scotia. Cold and distant, he watches me and the boys pack. When we drive off, he stays behind. A week later, I find a message in my email inbox from him and open it, glad to find him thinking of us. But it's not what I expect. I am completely confused to find him telling me that he is going to Cancun for a week with one of his old bachelor friends; and moreover, that the only reason he is telling me is because he engaged a friend of ours to cat-sit, and she told him that unless he told me himself, she was going to tell me.

A leaden weight settles over me. I had not imagined this level of deceit from him; it was bad enough that he had refused to accompany me and his sons on vacation, but then to arrange a separate vacation at his old stomping grounds of Cancun with a party buddy? "Dad is going to Cancun," I tell the boys, knowing I shouldn't share this with them but unable to help myself. They nod blankly and the day goes on.

That afternoon we are down on the beach and a dense white fog rolls in, so thick we can't see more than a couple of feet out to sea. The boys are snorkeling around the rocks in their wetsuits, looking for crabs. I wander up and down the beach in total fog, literally and figuratively, tears streaming down my face once again. I can't avoid the truth any longer: my marriage is over.

Still, somehow I continued to delude myself with the hope that he would repent and change his mind. All the long drive home from Nova Scotia, 18 hours in the car, I hoped and wished to find him loving and contrite when we returned, ready to make up and move forward together. When we arrived in the early evening, exhausted and hungry after nine hours on the road, he greeted us coldly and continued what he was doing: making a smoothie and getting his gym bag together. I asked him for a sip of his drink, being so hungry

I thought I might pass out. Reluctantly he handed me his glass, then quickly recovered it and drained it himself before bounding out the door with a careless wave, leaving us to unpack the car. Heartsick, I watched him go.

Later, when he told me about his plans to find an apartment and move out, I still tried to talk him into staying. "It's going to be very hard financially, you know," I said gently. "Are you sure you want to do this?"

Let me give you my ass so you can kick it harder. Yeah.

I am not proud of this passage in my life, but I don't want to lie about it, either. Sugar-coating it won't help.

The truth is that I was in denial, for a long, long time, about what was happening in my personal life. I too was playing a *"luz en la calle, oscuridad en su casa"* kind of role. There I was, teaching my women's studies classes about male privilege and women's resistance without ever admitting, even to myself, how abased I was in my own marriage. As the years of this went by, the disjunction between my values, my rhetoric and my reality became harder and harder to bear, but in the quest to maintain the appearance of conventional well-being I became a damned good liar and actor, capable of switching roles on a dime. Only years later did I recognize the toll this acting took on me as I alienated myself further and further from the core of who I once was.

For months I have been compulsively searching for dogs on the Internet, looking up different breeds, finding breeders, exploring rescue sites. All through the long years of marriage and parenting, I have not been especially interested in getting a dog—I've had my cat and that has been enough. But now I know, with the same kind of wordless certainty I had as a child when I insisted on getting Pushkin, that I must have a dog. I must have a companion who loves me completely, just as I am, without conditions or criticisms or nuance. I need a dog to pull me back out into the woods again, to get me away from my desk and back out into the healing green temple of the mountain forests. I need a dog to remind me of who I used to be, before I plunged into the stream of adult life and found my self-connection severed. I need a dog to lead me back home.

AIR

SHOCKED AWAKE
AT MIDLIFE

In the 21 years between my marriage and my divorce, I gave birth to and raised two sons, published two books and many articles, taught hundreds of classes in literature, writing, gender studies and media studies, and mentored dozens of students. For the most part, I followed a conventional path, with minor deviations: instead of marrying a nice Jewish boy, I married a Mexican; instead of teaching the Western canon, I taught literature by women of color; instead of doing whatever it would take to get a tenure-track academic job, I accepted part-time adjunct work, giving priority to my role as a mother. I regret none of these choices. No, the choice I regret is much further back in my history—the decision I made as a college student to give up on my solitary walks with chickadees in the woods, and focus my attention on the human landscape. As an adult, absorbed in the daily rhythm of nurturing my children, keeping up with my career and trying to maintain a relationship with my husband, I forgot, for a long time, what had been most fundamental to the core of my identity as a child: the old need I had to get outside regularly, to commune with the trees and other elements of the natural world. It took a series of shocks to force me to start remembering who I really was.

Gloria Anzaldúa always insisted that we need precipitating shocks to push us to move in new directions and grow. Her valorization of pain as a source of wisdom seemed strange to me at first, because I came from a family, and a culture, that always tried to avoid shocks of any kind—that held comfort as the highest value. Anzaldúa argues that without shocks we lose our creative edge and become complacent. It's not enough, she says, to experience trauma vicariously, as I had been doing with my reading of the painful personal narratives of other women, or as Euro-American culture does when we project our fascination with aggression and pain pornographically into the realm of re-presentation, flooding our media with constantly escalating images of violence even while we carefully construct walls around ourselves to keep us more "secure."

The shocks that are most valuable—that can, as Rumi recognized long ago, open a wound through which the light can enter—are the ones that we feel ourselves. The end of my marriage, painful as it was, proved to be a valuable personal catalyst for me, pushing me to look hard at so many things I had been doing my best, for many years, not to see. Living the tenuous life of an adjunct professor taught me firsthand about the need for structural change of this exploitative system, which I would not have understood as powerfully if I had coasted into a tenured professorship early in my career. I also learned about the particular pressures of the working mother by living through them, day by busy day, myself.

Shocks can be valuable on a planetary level too. A hurricane like Sandy galvanizes people to action, while the relatively slow melting of the polar ice or gradual increase in global temperatures doesn't, because it's still possible to practice avoidance and selective vision: dealing with a hot summer by adjusting the thermostat on the AC, like frogs sitting passively in the pot while the water comes slowly to a boil. That is an apt description of what the fire years were like for me. As things got less and less comfortable for me in my marriage and at work, I never seriously considered simply jumping out of the pot and changing my reality. I thought that if I just worked harder, I could make things right. It took some tough shocks to get me to see that I was not going to be able to find happiness if I limited myself to working within the same paradigm that was making me unhappy. I had to go deeper, and take the risk of real change.

For many years I had pored over women's stories of suffering, resistance and resilience—almost as though I was trying to learn, while still safe in my pampered, privileged gated community, how to survive the shocks that might await me. When Teo moved out and when, a year later, my university position was terminated by budget cuts, I began to feel the pinch of some real knocks of my own. The long magic carpet ride I'd been enjoying finally came to an end, and I couldn't lie to myself or to others any longer, pretending that everything was fine.

Everything was not fine. I was now a single mother, with an inadequate income, struggling to make ends meet. Yes, I still had my parents to fall back on—they were my bulwark against the full catastrophe that would have otherwise awaited me, as I could not have afforded to keep my house without their support. Buffeted by insecurity, I tried to keep myself focused on being the best parent I could be to my children, and forging ahead as best I could with my career. Looking around me, I saw many women in similar situations, doing their best while contending with structural impediments, both external and internalized, that often made life feel like an interminable session of swimming upstream against powerful currents.

In the wake of my divorce, I was able to understand as never before how being socialized as a woman, even in the seemingly progressive United

States, had held me back from stepping into my full human potential. I had been socialized to avoid confrontation; to go docilely with the flow; to trust in established systems and frameworks. I had played by the rules of the game, I thought, in my marriage and my career; but still I found myself at midlife living out the stark, uncomfortable story of the divorced and underemployed mother.

While these storms ploughed through my personal life, I also woke up to even bigger troubles that were brewing in the world. For the first time, I became aware of the looming, slow-motion crisis of climate change, the accelerating extinction of species, and the specter of human beings destroying the possibility of our own continued existence on Earth. Suddenly I was able to understand the strands of my own life story in a new way, seeing how completely dependent I, like every human, was on the benevolent support of Mother Earth. As a girl, I had instinctively gravitated to the loving embrace of Gaia, the living Earth; but as a young adult I had joined a powerful cultural stream that led me into an alienated relationship to the planet. I had reconnected somewhat through my children and their delight with the natural world; but for many years I had focused only on people and human concerns. Now it was time to step into the adult role that Gaia needed from me, becoming a steward of the planet—and to do so as a fully conscious woman, understanding how urgently women's perspectives are needed to counter the centuries of masculine ascendancy that had brought us to this 21st century juncture of environmental crisis. The time for playing by the rules was over. It was time to write a new playbook.

EARTH

ON SHIFTING GROUND

I am standing at the podium, squinting in the spotlight and looking out over the audience of more than a hundred people, gathered for the 10th annual International Women's Day conference that I have once again worked with a committee to organize. I've titled the event after one of my signature classes, "Women Write the World," and invited several inspiring women to take part: environmental writer Sandra Steingraber will give the keynote, talking about her anti-fracking campaign in New York State and her new film, Living Downstream; *the Native American author Deborah Miranda will read from her book* Bad Indians: A Tribal Memoir, *which intertwines personal and cultural history; and I've also organized a panel featuring co-editors and contributors to the new anthology I've co-edited,* African Women Writing Resistance. *It's going to be a rich, provocative program, and I'm excited for it to begin.*

*But first I have an offering of my own to make.
I've prepared a slide lecture called* Women Write
the World, *talking about women through the ages,
from Sheherezade and Christine de Pizan to Mary
Wollstonecraft and Harriet Jacobs, concluding with
an introduction to my heroines, Audre Lorde, Gloria
Anzaldúa and Rigoberta Menchú. I also include an
anecdote from my own life, sharing with the audience
how I began to try to use writing to right the world
when I was a child, writing the story of the wood
nymph Estrella, who set off on a quest to rescue the
forest from the loggers.*

*I am happy to note that my voice no longer shakes
with nervousness when I speak into the microphone.
I'm finally able to pull away from my written notes
and speak unscripted, from the heart. Although I'm
no closer to having an answer for how to stop the
destruction of the forest, at least I am moving out into
the world, seeking companions on the quest.*

*"The wisdom and power of women of the world
are needed desperately now," I conclude. "I reach back
to my 10-year-old self, grieving over the trees cut and
dying by the roadside, and extend a hand of comfort
and encouragement. Come now, let's go. We'll find
the answers together."*

From my early closeness with my mother and
my best friends Imin and Allison, to my graduate
school friends, to my many years of organizing academic and community events honoring women's

perspectives and achievements, I have always drawn the warmth of women around me like a cloak. Instinctively I knew, and my long feminist apprenticeship confirmed, that the way women understand and relate to the world is different—and that our Western worldview has been dominated by a perversion of the masculine warrior energies, channeled into domination and control instead of protection and partnership. Femininity has also been misunderstood to signify compliance and a focus on superficial beauty rather than substance.

Coming into midlife, I found myself drawn back to my college explorations of Virginia Woolf's theory that all human beings have the potential to be psychologically androgynous. This is true on a biological level too: all humans have both estrogen and testosterone running through our bloodstream, and where we fall on the spectrum of gender expression is a function of unique combinations of chemistry and social conditioning. More and more, I wanted to spend my time working to shift the social pressures that had made it difficult for me to embrace my own warrior nature. As a woman, I had found it hard to fight the conditioning that said I should be meek and quiet, both professionally and at home. In my work as an ally for other women—my teaching, writing and community organizing—I had been dedicated to helping women fight the barriers, both internal and external, that too often prevent us from getting our ideas and perspectives further out into the world. If more women were able to speak our truths in the public sphere, I thought, we might succeed in creating a more balanced culture, one that honored the feminine attribute of nurturing as much as the masculine quality of aggression.

As my marriage ended, I began a new phase of my life. Instead of anchoring myself to one person, or even to my one small family, I began to try to stitch together a larger family of kindred spirits, those who were also awake to the unfolding environmental crises, and seeking to align their personal and political values in harmony with the spiritual ecology of Gaia. At this point it seemed crucial to me that I get away from the alienation of academic-style discourse, and simply speak and write from my heart. I started a blog, *Transition Times*, experimenting with writing honestly and directly about the social and environmental challenges we face in our times. To my great joy, I found an almost instant response beaming back to me from people all over the world, who encouraged me to keep on going in my exploration of aligning the personal, political and planetary through writing. In one of my early posts, I drew on a metaphor from my experience as a mother to explain my choice of the title of the blog:

> Just before a baby is born, the laboring mother is said to be "in transition." This is what happens when the birth canal is dilating enough to allow the infant's big head to drop

down into the free air. Our world is in transition now, about to give birth to something new and different. We who are alive today, in these transition times, are the midwife and the laboring mother, as well as the baby about to be born. Our job is to love and nurture, to build a deep resilience so that we can survive and thrive in the new world that is coming. This is the work of my second half of life.

My commentary on national and world events was accompanied by a series of blog posts in which I tried to work through the tremendous sorrow and distress that often engulfed me during this time. My grief at the loss of my marriage blurred with my grief at the destruction of the natural world, shading into anger as I realized how I had allowed myself to become alienated from the deep inner guidance I had known as a child, my own passionate voice becoming strait-jacketed, over the years, by my fear of taking the risk of speaking and acting from the heart. I grieved for the death of the dream I had had when I married: that it would be forever, that Teo and I would get old happily side by side, nourishing and cherishing the spark that had brought us together. I grieved for the death of my childish faith that the authorities, those in charge, could be trusted to always have our best interests in mind. I grieved as I realized that while I wasn't paying attention, Gaia and her creatures had been suffering terribly from human mistreatment. I could no longer count on the places I loved to always be there, intact, waiting for me to return: the apple trees buzzing with bees, the chickadees trooping merrily through the hemlock woods, the stately maples reaching out their boughs to greet me. But it was the kind of grief that led to resolve: I was finally ready to balance within myself my loving, feminine energies with my masculine warrior spirit; ready to commit myself fully to task of nurturing that balance in other individuals, in our society, and in the ecological systems of our suffering, imbalanced planet herself.

It's Christmas Day and I'm feeling kind of blue. Even though Teo never liked or participated much in our family celebrations of Christmas, hanging back grumpily as I followed my mother's pattern of decorating the house and baking cookies and heaping presents under the tree, it still feels odd to go through a Christmas season without him in the picture. The weather is pleasant and there's still no snow on the ground, so after breakfast the boys and I decide to take a hike before we join my parents for dinner. They climb the mountain rapidly, our dog bounding around them, while I follow more slowly, trying to enjoy the peaceful forest trail, but feeling heavy-hearted and sad.

After a long incline, we come out on a ridge strewn with massive boulders, jumbled together roughly. The boys start climbing, ignoring my warning about the bears that may be dreaming away in the deep caves and

crevices. *I lean up against one of the towering rocks,
left here by some great glacier in its retreat down the
mountainside. Closing my eyes, it isn't hard to imagine
an even earlier time, when the rocks were home to
myriads of fish, with giant squid sleeping in the caves,
instead of snoring bears. These great rocks have seen
so much earthly history, standing majestically on their
mountainside, unmoved by the shallower destinies of
the flora and fauna that root on them or pass them by.*

*For a moment, putting my hand on the cold rough
stone, my inner turmoil is calmed by a strong apprehension of the longer view of life on Earth. These ancient
stones have seen upheavals far more intense than
what humankind is currently living through. They
have survived as silent witnesses to many cycles of
destruction and regeneration. They will be there, still
silently bearing witness, after Homo sapiens has
become just another footnote in the fossil record of the
planet. There is strange comfort in this.*

*Wanting to record this moment of clarity, I ask
my son to take a picture of me with my back up
against the powerful rock of ages. I know I look as
weathered and rough as the stone behind me; I can
feel the tension and exhaustion that is putting new
lines and wrinkles on my face. I don't care. It's not
a moment to worry about how I look for the camera.
It's a moment to affirm, staring into the unwinking
eye of the future, that I will dedicate the rest of my life
to trying to stave off destruction, not just for humans,
but for all beings on our planet.*

We head back down the mountain, my mood lightening a bit as I reflect that no matter how badly we may fail as a species, the planet will endure and the planet will evolve and find new ways of prospering, combining the building blocks of creation into wondrous, miraculously beautiful and clever forms. This knowledge forms a peaceful ledge on which to perch, quietly collecting my energy and my will for the struggles ahead.

When I turned 50, I didn't throw myself a big party, or even take my parents up on their offer of a plane ticket for a vacation. In the wake of the devastating strikes of Hurricanes Irene and Sandy, it seemed too frivolous to think about travel for pleasure. I had my usual quiet birthday dinner with my family, all of us straining a bit to find some shared joy in the moment.

During this time, I often caught myself thinking back, trying to remember what it felt like to be truly happy: the sense of exhilaration I used to get from walking the beach at Martha's Vineyard in the late afternoon; the deep sense of happiness that washed over me as a child when I stood on the ridge at dawn, listening to the first sleepy birds begin to sing and watching the rays of the sun stream golden over the mountains. I could remember the sensation of happiness, but I didn't seem to be able to summon that emotion now. It was as if some crucial emotional synapse had been severed in me. The best I could manage was a resigned contentment.

I wanted the symbolic year of 50 to mark a new beginning in my life, the start of a new era, in which I would no longer be weighed down and caged by how my life had unfolded over the past quarter-century. I wanted to roll back the clock to the time before I had allowed myself to be swayed from the intuitive certainties of my childhood by my teenaged desire to belong, to fit in, to join the conformist stream. I was haunted by the image of myself sitting in the woods writing furiously in my notebook about Estrella and the forest; I wanted to go back to the purity of vision I had had then, to the passionate conviction I had poured into my writing. I knew it was time to step up as a full adult in my society, ready to work with others in creating sustainable ways of living more lightly on the Earth. But I still felt a little uncertain of my own role in such a movement. I wasn't a scientist, or a politician. What did I really have to offer?

Finally, after much pondering, it came to me. What I had to offer was my own simple, ordinary life story. My story, like Rigoberta Menchú's, is also the story of my people. It is the story of a generation of Americans who grew up with tremendous privilege, so comfortable and coddled that we were not even aware of how very privileged we were. It is the story of many generations of Euramericans who grew up believing that they had the right to take endlessly from the natural world, without fear of exhausting the planet's resources, and without ever giving anything back. It is the story of my generation's tremendous alienation from Nature, our reliance on technology and engineering to solve all problems, to the point where we could delude ourselves that we did not need the natural world to make us happy, only our own representations of her, and the resources we could extract at the push of a button.

My story is the story of how finally, at midlife, I came back to my senses and woke up to the impending disaster that my generation had presided over unthinkingly. Although far from unique or special, my story, honestly told, could be sent out into the world like a beacon, helping me find others who were ready to tackle these transition times head on. Together we could undertake the great struggle of our time: the struggle to turn our tremendous human intelligence to the good work of creating a livable future for ourselves, our children and the millions of innocent species that are staring extinction in the face in these early years of the 21st century. Happiness could wait. It was resolve I needed now—courage and determination. I was only a small, flawed and limited woman—I was no great warrior, no heroine, no shining light. But such as I had to offer to the struggle, I would offer with an open heart.

EARTH/WATER/ FIRE/AIR

HEEDING GAIA'S CALL

It's a beautiful fall day, crisp and clear, the maples lighting up golden and red along the ridge. Walking slowly and pensively over the land my grandparents bought more than 50 years ago, I can feel the layering of time that nestles into each dip and rise.

There are the limestone outcroppings that my mother determinedly exposed with her spade and trowel, digging up the clods of soft wild grasses to reveal the strong bones of the land beneath. Now, her fully developed rock garden provides a long arm of stone and succulents stretching between the little house and the new big house that my parents built in 1989. On the other side of the little house, the ferns and Mayapples that I transplanted from the woods to make my woodland garden now carpet the slope beneath my old climbing tree, Cricket. I note that the branch I used to swing myself up on is gone, so that it would take a ladder to get up into the gnarly branches of Cricket now. Looking around at the thick green lawn, I can squint and still see the dense swamp dogwood thicket that grew here when my parents first built the little house. How pleased we were the day that we broke through with our loppers and made a path all the way to Cricket! Now my son and his girlfriend live in that house, the fourth generation of my family to move gladly on to this land and become its loving keepers.

Walking up the old driveway where Grandma Fannie used to take me on "nature walks" when I was a toddler, I pay silent homage to the oldest tree on the land, the huge and vigorous grandmother maple that grew by the site of the hunting cabin my grandparents renovated for their country cottage. Now that cottage has been torn down and rebuilt as a bright, airy pottery studio for my mom. She created gardens around it, carefully selecting shrubs and perennials of little interest to the deer that stroll out of the forest with their fawns each spring. This is where my childhood friend Allison and I would play our imaginary games, watched sleepily by the generations of owls that nested in Yggdrasil and the other sentinel maples on the ridge above the grassy Lower Meadow, full of wild strawberries, bee balm, goldenrod and asters.

This land, which I have loved since I was born, has responded to the solicitous tending of my family by becoming more beautiful and gracious year by *year. My parents' home, sitting on a high knoll looking out over the valley to the mountains in the distance, is the focal point for merry tribes of birds that come to their feeders year-round, nesting in the surrounding trees and bushes. Opossum, raccoons, rabbits, squirrels, chipmunks, deer, foxes, coyotes and the occasional bobcat crisscross through the fields and woods, intent on their own business. It's like a small Eden, proof that human beings can peacefully co-exist with nature, if we live in a loving relationship with the land we tend.*

At midlife I began to look backward over the spiral of my life. Needing to understand who I was, I wrote my way back to the girl who sat on a mossy boulder in the woods, writing intently in her notebook about the natural world; the girl who craved a dog companion; the young woman who searched single-mindedly for the partner with whom to start a family; the shy writer turned teacher...discovering that each of these earlier stages of myself had shaped the mature woman I now was, like the invisible rings on a tree reflecting its growth from year to year. It was essential for me to revisit my past in order to understand my present, and begin to envision my future. But more importantly, this journey has taught me that what's most interesting and valuable about my life is how it has intertwined with and been shaped by the lives of others and the great throbbing life of the natural world.

The calm, commanding face of Majesty, the regal tiger whose portrait I hung over my bed as an adolescent, is never far from my mind now. Even then, in my innocence, I knew that the spirit of the natural world represented by the tiger I named Majesty was calling on me to put the intelligence, skills and privilege I possessed as my human birthright at the service of those at the mercy of the shadow side of humanity—our rapacious greed, our cruelty and aggression. I don't believe it's coincidental that all my life I have been drawn to the wisdom of so-called "indigenous peoples," indigenous meaning that they have retained their close ties to the land of their ancestors, rather than rolling restlessly across the Earth as so many others have done. My ancestors cast themselves on the sea and headed for the New World to escape persecution, and I am grateful that they did. But I believe, with Jung and many others, that there is more to us humans than our physical ancestry would suggest. On a soul level, we have kinships and affinities that go far beyond the DNA that gives us physical shape; and even on the biological level, we are learning more and more about the common heritage of all life on Earth. We who have been brought up in what some call the "settler culture" or "the West" must begin to learn from the scattered and beleaguered remnants of the ancient indigenous peoples, who have never forgotten what we most need to remember now:

that unless we begin to live in harmony with each other and with our Mother Earth, we humans will go the way of the dinosaurs, shrugged off as a failed experiment while Gaia continues her patient and interminable work of creating abundant life on the planet.

On a sunny spring morning, I take a path I have not walked for many a year. Something is calling me up this steep mountain today, behind the cheerfully wagging tail of my dog. The jack-in-the-pulpit leaves are new and shiny beside the trail and the ferns are still slowly unfurling, the fiddleheads like thousands of question marks accompanying me up the mountain. As I approach the summit, panting with exertion, the rocks become slippery with spring ice, and I pick my way carefully to my destination: the wide, smooth stone outcropping, studded with gleaming white quartz, where long ago I sat and imagined a Mohican woman receiving a vision of Henry Hudson sailing up the big river towards her homeland. Sitting down in the same spot, facing the wide vista of the valley to the East, I wonder: was that just my imagination, or could I have tapped into a memory from the collective unconscious of this mountain and the people who have sought her wisdom throughout the centuries?

I sit quietly, my dog warm and peaceful beside me, and open myself up to Gaia as I have done instinctively since I was a child. I feel my heart energy rising to meet the bright sun streaming down on the top of my head, and the great solemn pulse of the mountain moving firm and steady up my spine. Show me the way, Gaia, I pray. Let me be a channel for your wisdom. Having come almost to the end of my biological role of mothering, I am ready to open my heart wider, to lavish my love, which is just a faint reflection of your great abundant Love, on all living beings. There is so much pain in the world now; humans are suffering, and humans are causing great suffering for other life forms. I know it doesn't have to be this way. We are born to dance with beauty and light, as you model for us in the wild places still left for us to visit and learn from. We humans can learn; that is one of our greatest strengths. I vow to you, Gaia, I will dedicate the rest of my life to the great work of helping others remember why we are here—not to consume and destroy, but to cherish and nurture, to use our tremendous intelligence in the service of greater beauty and happiness for all life on Earth.

I open my eyes and see a bald eagle soaring by far below me, out in the vista, its white head and tail feathers glistening unmistakably in the sun. Even through the distance separating us, I can feel the fierce energy of the great bird moving across the landscape unerringly, without hesitation or regret. A fitting symbol for the way I want to live the rest of my life, I think to myself as I follow the eagle with my eyes until it wheels out of sight. Let it be so.

As I come to the end of this narrative, I find myself landing back on the ground of my being, strongly rooted in my past and ready to continue growing; now mature and sturdy enough to offer myself as shelter for others coming along the path too. We are living through remarkable times, times of great transition. When I was born, a half-century ago, who would have imagined that the American President would be a Black man with an African father and white mother? That the Catholic Pope would be an environmental advocate? That solar panels and wind turbines would be a routine part of our landscape? That the wealthy countries would begin to pay the less developed nations to preserve their forests? That the Rights of Nature would be enshrined as international doctrine, with as much credibility as Human Rights?

There are grounds for great hope now, even though the daily barrage of bad news continues unabated. Taking a longer view, I can foresee a time when the feminine principle of nurturing will combine with the masculine principle of protection to usher in an era of balance and harmony on our planet—the bleak Anthropocene turned into a verdant Androgynocene as human wisdom and ingenuity, channeled into stewardship, make it possible for all to thrive in integral communion with the abundance of Gaia.

As my narrative moves in towards the present moment, I throw out my story like a rope bridge connecting to yours, for what is urgently needed now is that we come together to share in the great work of repairing our selves, our societies, and our world. How will you add your piece of mosaic to the great ongoing story of human life on earth? Will we work together to collectively create a work of harmony and beauty, like a great stained glass window or the living canvas of a remote wilderness? Or will our presence as humans on Earth leave behind only a post-apocalyptic rubbish heap? Contemporary pop culture very often shows us the latter vision, and we are at a crucial juncture now—the story could go either way. Which way will you choose? Just as chaos theory says that the wind from a butterfly's wings is felt throughout the world, you and I cannot predict, and should not underestimate, the personal and planetary effects of our small daily choices.

I am sitting with a small group of women, each of us intent on writing in her own notebook, but subtly generating a collective field of focused energy that is palpable in the cozy salon where we have gathered for the weekend memoir writing retreat I am leading. We have just read the beautiful Rilke sonnet that I learned from Joanna Macy, the one with the magical line for memoirists: "If the drink be bitter, turn your-self to wine." I write in my notebook:

It is rare, perhaps impossible, to arrive at midlife without having experienced moments of pain, suffering, bitterness. To be alive is to be exposed to the vagaries of a society that is often harsh and cruel to individuals; to have met with natural calamities and health disruptions; to have known disappointment and struggle. But without this complexity of experience, how bland and uninteresting we would be! Turning our lived experience to a wine or elixir that will be of benefit to others is the task of the purposeful memoirist. Like good wine, we improve with age, and have so much more to offer each other and our world. Let us ring out, from our bell towers of words, the strength we all need now.

As we go around the circle listening to how each of us has taken up the rope bridge cast out by Rilke and used it to carry his idea further into the future, into our own lived experiences, I feel so grateful to be a part of this weaving together of words and intentions, each of us working alchemically to make her life an offering to the great collective artwork that is our human gift to Gaia.

The psychologist Kaethe Weingarten says hope is a verb—and it assumes its most powerful form in the first person plural. I want to spend the rest of my life out in the forests and fields of Gaia, and in circles of thoughtful people, doing hope together: overcoming fear, moving beyond silence and creating for ourselves and our descendants the once and future heaven on Earth that we forgot, a long time ago, and must remember now.

ACKNOWLEDGMENTS

It takes a village to make a book, especially a memoir covering 50 years of life.

I offer thanks to my foremothers: the long chain of powerful women to whom I am related by biology or affinity, whose voices have animated and strengthened mine.

I thank the friends, family, allies and mentors who have walked parts of the journey with me; you have sustained me with your integrity, courage, competence, good sense and warmth.

Thanks to my students, who have inspired me as they've taught me that learning is always a collaborative process.

For my sons, I offer a *mea culpa* for taking so very long to wake up and look beyond the personal and the political to the planetary. Let's do hope together now and forever.

SUGGESTIONS FOR FURTHER READING

A personal, idiosyncratic and definitely not exhaustive list of books and films that have inspired me as I've explored the themes and issues in *What I Forgot...And Why I Remembered.*

Environmental Memoir

Daly, Mary. *Outercourse: The Be-dazzling Voyage.* 1998.

Ensler, Eve. *In the Body of the World: A Memoir of Cancer and Connection.* 2014.

Hill, Julia Butterfly. *The Legacy of Luna: The Story of a Woman, a Tree and the Struggle to Save the Redwoods.* 2001.

Maathai, Wangari. *Unbowed: A Memoir.* 2007.

Macdonald, Helen. *H is for Hawk.* 2014.

Macy, Joanna. *Widening Circles: A Memoir.* 2001.

McKibben, Bill. *Oil and Honey: The Education of an Unlikely Activist.* 2014.

Pipher, Mary. *The Green Boat: Reviving Ourselves in Our Capsized Culture.* 2013.

Steingraber, Sandra. *Living Downstream: An Ecologist's Personal Investigation of Cancer and the Environment.* 1997.

   – *Having Faith: An Ecologist's Journey to Motherhood.* 2003.

   – *Raising Elijah: Protecting Our Children in an Age of Environmental Crisis.* 2013.

Williams, Terry Tempest. *Refuge: An Unnatural History of Family and Place.* 1992.

   – *When Women Were Birds.* 2013.

Wilson, Diane. *Diary of an Eco-Outlaw: An Unreasonable Woman Breaks the Law for Mother Earth.* 2011.

Environmental Writing

Carson, Rachel. *The Sea Around Us.* 1951.

– *Silent Spring.* 1962.

– *The Sense of Wonder.* 1965.

Goodstein, Eban. *Fighting for Love in the Century of Extinction: How Passion and Politics Can Stop Global Warming.* 2007.

Hertsgaard, Mark. *Hot: Living Through the Next Fifty Years on Earth.* 2011.

Jensen, Derrick. *Endgame, Volume 1: The Problem of Civilization.* 2006.

– *Endgame, Volume II: Resistance.* 2006.

– *Dreams.* 2011.

Jensen, Derrick, Lierre Keith and Aric McBay. *Deep Green Resistance: Strategy to Save the Planet.* 2011.

Kimmerer, Robin Wall. *Braiding Sweetgrass: Indigenous Wisdom, Scientific Knowledge, and the Teachings of Plants.* 2013.

Kolbert, Elizabeth. *Field Notes from a Catastrophe.* 2010.

– *The Sixth Great Extinction: An Unnatural History.* 2015.

Klein, Naomi. *This Changes Everything: Capitalism vs. the Climate.* 2015.

Lappé, Frances Moore. *Eco-Mind: Changing the Way We Think, to Create the World We Want.* 2011.

– *Getting a Grip: Clarity, Creativity and Courage in a World Gone Mad.* 2007.

Lovelock, James. *The Revenge of Gaia: Earth's Climate Crisis and the Fate of Humanity.* 2007.

– *The Vanishing Face of Gaia: A Final Warning.* 2009.

Macy, Joanna. *Active Hope: How to Face the Mess We're In Without Going Crazy.* 2012.

– *World As Lover, World As Self: Courage for Global Justice and Ecological Renewal.* 2007.

Macy, Joanna and Molly Brown. *Coming Back to Life: Practices to Reconnect Our Lives, Our World.* Second Edition. 2014.

— *Pass It On: Five Stories That Can Change the World.* 2010.

Marcos, Subcommandante. *Our Word is Our Weapon.* 2002.

McKibben, Bill. *Eaarth: Making a Life on a Tough New Planet.* 2011.

Moore, Kathleen Dean. *Moral Ground: Ethical Action for a Planet in Peril.* 2011.

Rifkin, Jeremy. *The Empathic Civilization: The Race to Global Consciousness in a World in Crisis.* 2009.

— *The Third Industrial Revolution: How Lateral Power is Transforming Energy, the Economy and the World.* 2011.

Shiva, Vandana. *Earth Democracy: Justice, Sustainability and Peace.* 2005.

Simons, Nina. *Moonrise: The Power of Women Leading from the Heart.* 2010.

Starhawk. *Webs of Power.* 2008.

Wheatley, Margaret. *So Far From Home: Lost and Found in Our Brave New World.* 2012.

– *Finding Our Way: Leadership for an Uncertain Time.* 2007.

Williams, Terry Tempest. *The Open Space of Democracy.* 2010.

Environmental Speculative Literature

Atwood, Margaret. *The Handmaid's Tale.* 1998.

Callenbach, Ernest. *Ecotopia.* 2004.

Starhawk. *The Fifth Sacred Thing.* 1994.

Spiritual Ecology

Allen, Paula Gunn. *The Sacred Hoop: Recovering the Feminine in American Indian Traditions.* 1992.

– *Grandmothers of the Light: A Medicine Woman's Sourcebook.* 1992.

Baring, Anne. *The Dream of the Cosmos.* 2013.

– *Soul Power: An Agenda for a Conscious Humanity.* 2009.

Berry, Thomas. *The Dream of the Earth.* 2006.

– *The Great Work: Our Way into the Future.* 1999.

Chodron, Pema. *The Places That Scare You: A Guide to Fearlessness in Difficult Times.* 2002.

– *Taking the Leap: Freeing Ourselves From Old Habits and Fears.* 2010.

Daly, Mary. *Quintessence: Realizing the Archaic Future.* 1999.

Gill, Penny. *What in the World is Going On? Wisdom Teachings for Our Time.* 2015.

Hanh, Thich Nhat. *Love Letter to the Earth.* 2013.

Lushwala, Arkan. *The Time of the Black Jaguar: An Offering of Indigenous Wisdom for the Continuity of Life on Earth.* 2012.

McErlane, Sharon. *A Call to Power: The Grandmothers Speak.* 2005.

McKenna, Terence. *True Hallucinations.* 1994.

Perkins, John. *Shapeshifting: Shamanic Techniques for Personal and Global Transformation.* 1997.

— The World Is As You Dream It: Teachings from the Amazon and the Andes. 1994.

Prechtel, Martin. The Unlikely Peace at Cuchumaquic: The Parallel Lives of People as Plants: Keeping the Seeds Alive. 2012.

Sarris, Greg. Mabel McKay: Weaving the Dream. 1994.

Silko, Leslie Marmon. Ceremony. 1977.

Starhawk. The Spiral Dance: A Rebirth of the Ancient Religion of the Goddess. 1979.

— Dreaming the Dark. 1997.

Swimme, Brian and Mary Ellen Tucker. Journey of the Universe: An Epic Story of Cosmic, Earth and Human Transformation. 2011.

Vaughan-Lee, Llewellyn. The Return of the Feminine and the World Soul. 2009.

— ed. Spiritual Ecology: The Cry of the Earth. 2013.

Women's Human Rights and Global Feminisms

Anzaldúa, Gloria. *Borderlands/la frontera: The New Mestiza.* 1987.

Anzaldúa, Gloria and Ana-Louise Keating, eds. *This Bridge We Call Home: Radical Visions for Transformation.* 2002.

Browdy de Hernandez, Jennifer, ed. *Women Writing Resistance: Essays on Latin America and the Caribbean.* 2004.

Browdy de Hernandez, Jennifer, Pauline Dongala, Omotayo Jolaosho and Anne Serafin, eds. *African Women Writing Resistance: Contemporary Voices.* 2010.

El Saadawi, Nawal. *The Nawal El Saadawi Reader.* 1997.

Galeano, Eduardo. *Open Veins of Latin America: Five Centuries of the Pillage of a Continent.* Monthly Review Press, 1971.

Hogan, Linda. *The Woman Who Watches Over the World: A Native Memoir.* 2002.

Lorde, Audre. *Sister Outsider: Essays.* 1984.

– *Zami: A New Spelling of My Name.* 1982.

Menchu, Rigoberta with Elisabeth Burgos-Debray.
 I, Rigoberta Menchu. 1983.

 − *Crossing Borders.* 1998.

Miranda, Deborah. *Bad Indians: A Tribal Memoir.* 2013.

Moraga, Cherrie and Gloria Anzaldúa, eds. *This
 Bridge Called My Back: Writings by Radical
 Women of Color.* 1981.

Partnoy, Alicia. *The Little School: Tales of
 Disappearance and Survival.* 1986.

Randall, Margaret. *Gathering Rage: The Failure of the
 20th Century Revolutions to Develop a Feminist
 Agenda.* 1999.

 − *When I Look Into the Mirror and See You: Women,
 Terror and Resistance.* 2002.

 − *Narrative of Power: Essays for an Endangered
 Century.* 2003.

Roy, Arundhati. *An Ordinary Person's Guide to
 Empire.* 2004.

Smith, Andrea. *Conquest: Sexual Violence and
 American Indian Genocide.* 2005.

Walker, Alice. *Possessing the Secret of Joy.* 1992.

Woolf, Virginia. *A Room of One's Own.* 1929.

— *Three Guineas.* 1938.

Writing Advice

Aronie, Nancy Slonim. *Writing From the Heart.* 1998.

Elbow, Peter. *Writing Without Teachers.* 1953.

Goldberg, Natalie. *Old Friend From Far Away: The Practice of Writing Memoir.* 2002.

— *Wild Mind: Living the Writer's Life.* 1990.

— *Writing Down the Bones: Freeing the Writer Within.* 1986.

Pipher, Mary. *Writing to Change the World.* 2007.

Environmental documentary and feature films

THE DAY AFTER TOMORROW (2004)

AN INCONVENIENT TRUTH (2006)

TAKING ROOT: THE VISION OF WANGARI
  MAATHAI (2008)

WALL-E (2008)

AVATAR (2009)

BAG IT (2010)

THE ECONOMICS OF HAPPINESS (2011)

CHASING ICE (2012)

MIDWAY (2013)

DO THE MATH (2013)

SYMPHONY OF THE SOIL (2013)

THIS CHANGES EVERYTHING (2015)

ABOUT THE AUTHOR

Jennifer Browdy is a writer, teacher, community organizer and public speaker with a passion for social and environmental justice.

She earned her Ph.D. in Comparative Literature at New York University and has taught world literature, gender studies, media studies, and environmental and social justice advocacy through writing and digital media strategies for more than 20 years at the college level.

Long committed to women's human rights and social justice, she directed a major annual conference in observance of International Women's Day for more than a decade, and works constantly and collaboratively to nourish and celebrate the voices and visions of women and girls.

Jennifer has published widely and spoken on the politics and poetics of social and environmental justice at many college campuses and conferences. In the coming years, she is looking forward to leading other women down the elemental path of purposeful memoir, working to strengthen the voices and visions of women of all ages, so we can step into our potential as the creative leaders the world needs now.

For more information on Jennifer's lectures, workshops, developmental editing and author coaching, visit JenniferBrowdy.com.

THE ELEMENTAL JOURNEY OF
PURPOSEFUL MEMOIR
A WRITER'S
COMPANION

JENNIFER BROWDY

You may also enjoy:

The Elemental Journey of Purposeful Memoir: A Writer's Companion

Using the four elements as a framework, 12 months of writing prompts unfold, offering guidance and encouragement on the journey to creating your own purposeful memoir. You don't have to "be a writer" to undertake this important inner work of looking back over your experience to understand where you are and to envision where you want to go—on a personal, political and planetary level.

Available now from Green Fire Press
Greenfirepress.com